GOR
£1·50

WITHDRAWN
FOR SALE

KU-362-173

WITHDRAWN
FOR SALE

WITHDRAWN
FOR SALE

THE GOOD STUFF

THE GOOD STUFF

LUCINDA MILLER

SB

To my children, Barney, Lara and Charlie.
You are my inspiration for this book
and my very special health heroes.
I will always love you to the moon and back.

Disclaimer: The information contained in this book is provided for general purposes only. It is not intended as, and should not be relied upon as, medical advice. The publisher and author are not responsible for any specific health needs that may require medical supervision. If you or your family have underlying health problems, or have any doubts about the advice contained in this book, you should contact a qualified medical, dietary or appropriate professional. While in some instances the author has provided suggestions for alternatives to common allergens, if you or your family have any allergies or require foods free of certain allergens please carefully check recipe ingredients and the labels of the products you are using. Neither the author nor the publisher can be held responsible for any claim or damage arising out of the use, or misuse, of the information and suggestions made in this book.

Published in 2018 by Short Books
Unit 316, ScreenWorks,
22 Highbury Grove
London, N5 2ER

10 9 8 7 6 5 4 3 2

Copyright © Lucinda Miller 2018

Lucinda Miller has asserted her right under the Copyright, Designs and Patents Act 1988 to be identified as the author of this work. All rights reserved. No part of this publication may be reproduced, stored in a retrieval system or transmitted in any form, or by any means (electronic, mechanical, or otherwise) without the prior written permission of both the copyright owners and the publisher.

A CIP catalogue record for this book is available from the British Library.

ISBN: 978-1-78072-355-6
Cover and book design by Smith & Gilmour
Photographs copyright ©Andrew Burton
Food stylist: Emily Jonzen
Props stylist: Olivia Wardle
Additional photographs by Daniela Exley (pages 90, 116, 140)
and Millie Pilkington (front cover photo and pages 2, 6, 39, 62, 64, 92)

Printed in Slovenia by DZS Grafik, d.o.o.

CONTENTS

ALL ABOUT THE GOOD STUFF

RECIPES & MEAL PLANNERS

INTRODUCTION

WHAT IS HEALTHY?

If you ask 10 children what they think being healthy is, you'll probably get 10 different answers. For me, it all boils down to happiness. I'm convinced that, when you nourish bodies, minds and souls with proper food, you are building the health and resilience everyone needs to stay happy and well, even when life sends its inevitable challenges.

As new parents, we all set out with the grand intention of giving our children the best possible start in life, and at the heart of this is feeding them well. We imagine a glossy picture of a smiling family tucking into a delicious, home-cooked meal. The reality, of course, is rarely so perfect. For many families, even getting everyone to sit round a table together can be difficult enough, and when they do, dealing with all the family's likes and dislikes can turn mealtimes into a battleground.

SO WHERE DOES IT START TO GO WRONG?

For most parents, feeding a young baby their first foods is quite straightforward. It certainly felt like a walk in the park to me compared with the complications of birth, establishing breastfeeding and simply getting enough sleep.

It is usually during the 10- to 18-month stage, when a child begins to exhibit signs of independence, that the trouble starts. Young children are always looking for an opportunity to test boundaries and they soon learn that throwing their plate on the floor, spitting out food or clamping their lips together after a few mouthfuls are superb ways to get attention.

I will never forget my daughter, aged 10 months, having a wonderful time at her older brother's birthday party, eating everything from carrot sticks to sandwiches and cupcakes. That was her first introduction to anything more than mushed-up baby food and simple finger food. She had always been a fantastic eater and she really went for it.

The next day at breakfast, I produced her favourite porridge but madam wouldn't eat a single mouthful. She did the same with her stew at lunchtime and again at teatime, rejecting anything that had been puréed. This carried on for several weeks, and I got very worried.

Despite my training in nutrition, I was totally unprepared in those early days for the emotions involved in getting my children's feeding right. I still remember the sense of rejection when they refused to eat my lovingly prepared offerings. And I admit there were many times when the dog ate more of the children's food than they did.

I gradually learnt clever ways to help meal times go more smoothly. But each new stage brings fresh challenges. Older kids can be heavily influenced by their friends and the culture and the media they are exposed to, particularly when it comes to food. In fact, teenagers often need as much help as toddlers to get their food choices right – to learn to nourish themselves and have a positive, long-term relationship with what they eat.

IF YOU DON'T EAT YOUR GREENS...

It sounds obvious that we should give our children a healthy diet, but why is this so important?

You might think, given the number of celebrity chefs and cooking programmes on television today, that as a society we've never eaten better. But, sadly, it's far from true. The average modern diet, ever squeezed by our increasingly busy lives, is focused more on convenience than nourishment.

While our parents and grandparents mainly bought fresh, local ingredients and cooked their meals from scratch, we now fill more than half of our supermarket shopping trollies with ultra-processed foods that give us a quick fix of energy and taste[1].

It's as if nutrition from real food has been forgotten, despite everything we have learned from modern science about how crucial it is, especially for children. Proper nutrition is vital for strong immunity, for healthy teeth, for learning and development, for an easy puberty[2] and for maintaining a healthy weight.

Britain has reached a worrying record for childhood obesity[3]. And one of the primary causes for this is ultra-processed foods made from ingredients you won't find in a domestic kitchen: modified starches, hydrogenated fats, flavourings, emulsifiers and far too much refined sugar.

The government, rightly concerned, has introduced new guidelines[4] stating that, among other things, children should limit their added sugar intake to 19–30g per day, depending on their age. This is harder than you might think. Average intake is around double that, and a child may have eaten their entire day's sugar allowance[5] even before they leave the house in the morning.

At the same time, many kids hardly eat any veg at all; and nearly a third of the veg they do eat is highly-processed, coming from foods like pizza and baked beans. In a recent poll of 2,000 parents, more than 40% said they had abandoned any attempt to get greens into their kids[6].

Even parents who believe they are quite conscientious about their family's nutrition tend to be offering a far narrower diet than they realise. When a child has started refusing anything vaguely new or different, it is much easier to stick to the usual suspects – cereal, bread, carrots, cucumber sticks, apple juice, ham, chicken, pasta and cheese.

And this lack of variety matters. To maintain a healthy gut, which is now known to be crucial to robust physical and mental health, we need to eat as diverse a diet as possible: this is how we support the good bacteria in the gut microbiome which have a strong influence on our immune system and mood.

As it is, our impoverished low-fibre, high-sugar diet is setting up young people for all sorts of future health problems and it is thought to be a key cause of chronic bodily inflammation[7]. Ultra-processed foods can damage our metabolism[8] and contribute to diseases, including type 1 diabetes, coeliac disease[9], type 2 diabetes[10] and many cancers[11]. Both diabetes and coeliac disease are prevalent in my own close and extended family; and I have seen first-hand how much harder and more complicated life is for those who are affected.

Chronic inflammation can also impact on our mood[12] and cause serious mental health issues[13]. We now know that signs of inflammation at the age of nine can be a predictor for depression in the late teens[14]; while a recent study has established that a quarter of 14-year-old girls in the UK today suffer from symptoms of depression[15].

These are very unhappy statistics. If we are what we eat, this is arguably never truer than in our children, who are laying down the foundations for their long-term health.

IT'S NEVER TOO LATE TO EMBRACE THE GOOD STUFF

More positively, a recent study of children aged two to nine years old[16] showed that 'healthy eating is associated with better self-esteem and fewer emotional and peer problems, such as having fewer friends or being picked on or bullied.' The same findings of greater happiness and wellbeing have been confirmed in teenage studies[17–19].

The adolescent brain is still maturing well into the mid-20s[20], so it is never too late to start educating your kids on why positive nutrition is so important for mind and body.

We are exposed to very real dietary pressures in the modern world. Sugary and ultra-processed foods are everywhere, tempting us to grab them off the shelves. And yet, ironically, with air freight and new farming technology, we also have better year-round access to good fresh ingredients than ever before. I strongly believe that we shouldn't just cave in to marketing and pester power and let unhealthy convenience food become a habit.

The good news is that, whatever your child's age, with patience and persistence you *can* bring about change. During 20 years in clinical practice and nearly as many as a mother, I have built up a whole arsenal of strategies to encourage good eating habits in children – and I will be sharing these with you in this book.

MY STORY – MY HEALTH HEROES

During my life I have had many eureka moments about the incredible powers of nutrition, and the first was a very personal one. Up until my teens my health had been pretty good, but at university my energy levels dived and I slept through almost every single lecture. I revised in between naps and just squeezed a degree through. After university I landed a high-pressure job as an analyst in the city. By this point I also had bad gut problems and my periods only came a few times a year. Eventually, very weak and in pain, I crawled in to see a gastroenterologist, who shrugged it off as IBS, saying I would have to learn to live with it.

One day, after working through the weekend, I crashed in front of my boss. I was beyond exhausted. The company GP said my blood tests were OK and nothing more could be done. This is when a colleague suggested I go and see a naturopath. It *had* to be worth a try.

This appointment transformed my life. Out went the diet cola and fat-free yoghurt for breakfast, in came a diet of whole foods, good protein, fruit and veg. Within weeks, I was a different person, half a stone lighter, bouncing out of bed at 5.30am and no naps needed.

Slowly over the next few months, the myriad of niggly symptoms started to disappear. It was so transformational that, at my follow-up appointment, all I wanted to know was where to train as a naturopath. I duly enrolled on a course with the Holistic Health College, and since then I have studied at the Functional Medicine University, which has allowed me to practise a more integrated and evidence-based approach.

I am now a mother of three gorgeous kids. But, as for most parents, it hasn't always been easy. My eldest son had some co-ordination problems which affected his writing and organisation, and some chronic bowel issues. I knew from my training that there was a close link between diet, gut health and child development. This research was still in its infancy then, but it is now one of the most important areas of medical study.

We introduced some probiotics to my son's diet, along with some other simple interventions, all of which had a very positive effect. Over the next month, he made many big leaps at school, particularly in his written work. He also had a breakthrough making friends. Even more amazing, he started to hug us, having previously found it difficult to be physically close. These were special times for us all.

As his gut problems improved, so did his brain capacity and focus. A year or so later we had his IQ checked and it had gone up by nearly 20 points! A special educational needs school was no longer on the agenda. I am glad to report that he is now a healthy, sociable 17-year-old studying for A-levels.

Our youngest was a calm, adorable newborn who slept well from day one. However, three weeks into life he started being sick. Not just spitting up but projectile vomiting. We soon discovered that the pyloric valve of his stomach was half-closed, blocking the milk from nourishing him. At just seven weeks old he had an operation, after which he began to grow, but not as fast as we or our doctor had hoped.

Our paediatrician wanted to put him on a cocktail of medicines but first, preferring to try a more natural option, we pushed for a milk alternative and within two days he had stopped being sick. We kept him dairy-free for quite a while, as every time we tried feeding him even a small amount, it would all come back up again within minutes.

When he was 18 months old, I tried feeding him buffalo milk, having read that the proteins in it were more digestible. He glugged it down. We watched him over the next few days: no sickness and his nappies were better than normal. As he grew and glowed, we knew buffalo milk, or as he called it, 'gruffalo mulk', was the right thing for him. We also gave him probiotics and lots of gut-friendly foods, such as chicken soup and different fruits and veggies, and by the age of three he was able to tolerate all dairy. His gut may have matured naturally to achieve this, but I think it was down to having given his gut a break. I have learnt from supporting many more patients since then, that holding off from foods that are causing problems can give the body a chance to reset itself.

I was so confident by this point that we had ironed out any health issues that it was a huge shock when our daughter's health plummeted aged eight. My number two child, our beautiful girl, had been lucky with her health up until then. It was very frightening when she suddenly looked ashen grey and became exhausted, with aching joints and flu-like symptoms. Lights bothered her and, it seemed, almost overnight her memory and concentration deteriorated.

It turned out she had Lyme disease, which is a nasty bacterial infection from a tick bite. She was put on strong antibiotics and we took a fully integrated approach to help her immune system fight it. A carefully balanced diet rich in probiotics was the backbone and, happily for us, her health and energy bounced back.

Seeing my own children overcome their health challenges and blossom inspired me to start spreading the word that targeted nutrition can really make a huge difference. Specialising in paediatric naturopathic nutrition, I now look after well over 2,000 kids who have all manner of health challenges, from sore tummies and itchy skin to significant learning, behavioural and mental health issues. I receive emails all the time from grateful parents proudly telling me that their child has just spoken their first sentence, slept through the night or avoided sick days off school. I call them my little heroes and throughout this book I have told some of their inspiring stories.

THE GOOD STUFF VALUES

1 COOK FROM SCRATCH

A growing body of medical research is supportive of the health benefits of fresh food prepared from scratch. My number one aim is to get parents to roll up their sleeves and make cooking a priority and a joy in their household. Remember that processed foods include more than just burgers and chicken nuggets. There are lots of nasties – in particular, refined white sugar – hidden in seemingly benign items, such as cereals, yoghurts, fruit cordials and even bread. Keep it simple by buying ingredients rather than prepared convenience food and you can't go far wrong.

2 STICK TO WHOLE FOODS

I often get asked in my clinic what whole foods are and the answer is actually very simple: they are foods in their natural form; foods which have not been refined, processed or messed about with in any way. So, try to choose bread made from wholemeal flour, wholegrain brown rice and wholemeal or spelt pasta. Also use as many nuts, seeds, beans and pulses as you can in your cooking. Full-fat milk, cheeses and natural yoghurts are also whole foods and very important ones, too.

3 MORE FRUIT AND VEGETABLES

Remember the '5 a day' campaign launched by the UK department of health in 2002? Despite this, 80% of our kids and 95% of teenagers[21] are still fruit and veg dodgers. Children need to develop a taste for vegetables at an early age (ideally, 6–24 months) and they often need to be repeatedly exposed to these tastes (10–15 times) before they like them[22] – but I assure you it's worth it. You'll be setting them up with good habits for life. Remember, it is never too late to become a fruit and veg lover, and a taste for the fresh stuff can be re-ignited at any point in life. Older kids and even teenagers can easily be converted back to 5 (or more) a day if they understand why this is crucial to health and happiness.

4 MAKE IT DELICIOUS

If you want your children to be adventurous and curious about new foods and tastes, it is essential to make sure that whatever you offer them is tasty! Unfortunately, much of our baseline food is not as flavoursome or nutritious as it used to be. This is one of the reasons why food manufacturers fill their products with additional flavourings. So, if you can afford it, it is worth going the extra mile to seek out locally sourced and, ideally, organic food that tastes good naturally.

If you do want to boost flavour in a particular food, there are a whole host of healthy ways to do this: fresh and dried herbs, spices, garlic, lemon zest, anchovy paste, fish sauce, a touch of chilli, and a pinch of sea salt or black pepper can naturally turn a bland meal into a taste sensation.

5 VARIETY IS KEY

It is now clear that variety sows the seeds for a healthier life. Research has found that a healthy gut microbiome thrives on a huge range of different plant-based foods[23]. And, the greater the variety of fibre-rich foods your child eats, the healthier they are going to be.

Many children live off foods made from a very narrow set of ingredients – the most common culprits being wheat, milk products, soya, corn, sugar and tomatoes – which, in turn, limits the range of nutrients they get on a daily basis and also reduces the diversity of microbes in the gut.

Allergies and intolerances are on the rise, and this can also narrow down the range of food a child eats. At the same time, we are bombarded by the media with confusing messages about the food choices we should be making for our families. My advice is that, unless you know your child has a specific reason to remove certain foods from their diet, I urge you to view foodstuffs in their natural form as nourishing by default, as this will reflect positively on your child's relationship with food both in the short and long term.

Kids from every religious, ethnic and cultural background attend my clinic and they have shown me what a diverse diet the world offers and how flexible children's eating habits can be. Remember, a breakfast of sugary corn flakes is only typical to a small percentage of the world; a morning feast of eggs, soup, rice and vegetables is much more common than you might think. And far healthier too.

THE GOOD STUFF MANTRA

- Home-cooked is best
- Avoid processed foods
- Introduce more fruit and veg
- Make it tasty!
- Variety sows the seeds for a healthier life

WINNING WITH FRUITS & VEGGIES

Children, as we know, should be consuming a minimum of 5 portions of fruit and veg every day but what is less well-known is the importance of eating a wide variety of the fresh stuff[24]. I usually recommend at least 20 *different* raw or cooked plant-based foods per week for kids as this means they are more likely to get the range of vitamins, polyphenols and fibre they need to keep healthy. This might seem a little overwhelming at first, but to make it easier, I have included dozens of delicious plant-based recipes in this book, of which you will only need to cook a few each week to reach the golden 20.

The new thinking is that veg is considerably healthier than fruit due to fruit's higher sugar content; some people also warn of the risk of eating too much fructose. However, I think that fruit has lots of other nutritional benefits, such as providing vitamin C, polyphenols and fibre. As long as you get the balance right, and generally sway more towards vegetables, you will be heading in the right direction. Ideally the ratio should be at least three vegetables to two servings of fruit, rather than the other way around. But some fruit is still better than no fruit and veg at all.

HOW TO ENCOURAGE VEGGIE EATING

✳ **Introduce new foods one by one.** See it as a long-term programme rather than day-by-day or meal-by-meal. Pushing them too quickly can often backfire. Above all, remember to praise good results.

✳ **Think alternate bites:** one bite of a liked, known food, followed by one bite of a new food. You can then build up to two or three bites of the new food in a row.

✳ **Try foods in different forms and shapes.** For instance, if carrot discs are a no-no, try carrot batons, carrot purée, mashed carrot, roasted carrot or carrot juice; you may find a form that your child really loves.

✳ **If you have a child who will only eat off a segmented plate,** then just put a little of the new food in one segment, keeping the other known and loved foods 'safe' from the newcomer.

CLEVER WAYS TO HIDE VEG

1 GET GRATING

This is the easiest way to slip some secret veg into almost any meal. Simply grate a courgette or carrot into bolognaise, meatballs or stews when softening the onion.

2 PERFECT PURÉE

With really stubborn veg refusers, you may need to start from scratch with vegetable purées concealed within a food they like. Store the purées in the freezer in small quantities such as in an ice tray. Begin by adding 1–2 teaspoons of the puréed veg and then slowly add in a little more each time.

White veg combo
How to make it – Steam a mixture of potato, celeriac and cauliflower until soft. Blend with the remaining steam water or freshly made stock.
How to use it – Add to pancakes, muffins, waffles and bread recipes. This is a good starter purée for those who will only eat white/beige food.

Red veg combo
How to make it – Fry a mixture of red pepper, swede, courgette and red onion lightly in olive oil and purée it.
How to use it – Add to tomato sauces, curries, soups, meatballs, bolognaise or even to spaghetti rings or baked beans.

Green veg combo
How to make it – Steam turnip, cauliflower, courgette, broccoli and spinach. Blend with a little of the steam water or stock.
How to use it – Add to pancakes, mashed potato, fish cakes, curries, shepherd's pie, fish pie or even pesto.

Orange veg combo
How to make it – Steam carrot, butternut squash, orange pepper, cauliflower and swede. Blend with a little of the steam water or stock.
How to use it – Add to bolognaise, meatballs, shepherd's pie and stews as well as tomato sauces.

3 MIGHTY MASH

Mashed root vegetables such as carrot, squash, sweet potato, celeriac and swede are good alternatives to potatoes. Start adding a small amount to normal mash. See page 120 for my swede and potato topping in *Five Veg Shepherd's Pie.*

4 NICE 'RICE'

Cauliflower 'rice' is very easy to make if you have a food processor. Remove the tough central stalk from the cauliflower and pulse the florets 10–15 times until they are reduced to tiny rice/couscous-sized grains. Stir-fry in olive oil, coconut oil or ghee with a couple of tablespoons of water and add herbs or spices to taste. A good trick is to mix one teaspoon of cauli 'rice' into a serving of rice or couscous. Build up slowly and you might be able to replace the rice or couscous entirely.

5 NO-NONSENSE 'NOODLES'

These are made from spiralized or julienned vegetables, such as carrots, sweet potato, butternut squash and courgettes . You can serve them raw or gently fried in olive or coconut oil and garlic with basil.

6 'CRISPS' AND 'CHIPS'

Sweet potato, butternut squash and celeriac make delicious, guilt-free chips. See page 130 for my *Smart Sweet Potato Chips.* For crisps, a mandolin is crucial as the slices need to be extremely fine – a manual one will do, or some food processers come with mandolin blades. To get them really crispy, soak the slices in water for at least 10 minutes before patting them dry with a clean tea towel. Brush them lightly with coconut or olive oil, herbs and salt, then pop them in an oven preheated to 180°C/160°C fan/gas mark 4 for 7–8 minutes. Crispy kale is also quick and easy to make: strip off the woody stalks, toss the leaves in some olive oil and pop them in a hot oven for 8–10 minutes, shaking the baking tray now and then to stop them burning.

7 JUICES AND SMOOTHIES

Juicing helps your child absorb nutrients, partly because the process 'pre-digests' the ingredients. To make smoothies you can blend softer fruits and vegetables or salad leaves in a high-speed blender with some almond or coconut milk. See page 95.

8 LET THEM EAT CAKE!

Muffins are a great way to hide vegetables. Finely grate the veg into the muffin mix before adding a favourite flavour. Try my *Blueberry & Banana Muffins* on page 77. Brownies are also lovely and squidgy with added veg. Check out the *Courgette Brownies* on page 194.

LITTLE HERO: REUBEN

Reuben, aged 3, was one of the fussiest eaters I had ever met. His mum, Hannah, loved to cook healthy food which her other children enjoyed, but Reuben refused to eat anything resembling a vegetable. He only ate beige, crunchy food (dry cereal, nuggets, chips, toast and crackers), and only drank fruit juice.

Reuben is on the autistic spectrum and when he came to see me he had very little speech. Unknown foods were usually rejected with a meltdown that would last for hours, which made life in their household very difficult.

With some initial guidance from me, Hannah invested in a high-speed blender and started to experiment with recipes containing concealed fruits, vegetables, proteins and healthy fats. She made cookies with grated carrot or courgette. Soon he was also accepting waffles and pancakes and then she was able to add in my veg combo purées. Slowly but surely, Reuben's tastebuds changed and this has impacted on many areas of his life. He is now attending mainstream school and the entire family remain on his supercharged healthy diet.

CARBS WITHOUT THE SUGAR RUSH

We now have a generation of kids who are overweight and increasingly beset by wider physical and mental health problems. For instance, did you know that processed foods, such as biscuits, sweet cereals and cakes, can lower a child's immune system[25]? One study showed that our white blood cells' capacity to protect us from bacterial infection is significantly reduced after the consumption of sugar[26]. And this is to say nothing of rotting teeth. It is crazy to think that with our great dental care in the UK, a quarter of five-year-olds have tooth decay. A little bit of sugar is fine as an occasional treat, but it is hidden in everything from bread to ready-made sauces so it's not just sweets and chocolates that you have to wary of.

Every single carbohydrate source, from oatcakes to ice cream, can affect our blood sugar in some way, and in this book I look not just at added sugar but at the wider impact of carbohydrates on our health and metabolism[27], and which foods cause more problems than others.

THE GIST OF GI AND GL

The standard measure of how different foods affect our blood sugar is the Glycaemic Index (GI), which identifies how quickly a carbohydrate is digested and released as glucose (sugar) into our bloodstream. GI measures food from 0–100 and uses glucose, which has a GI of 100, as the reference point. Foods containing slowly absorbed carbohydrates have a low GI rating (55 or below) and include most fruits and vegetables, milk and some wholegrain cereals and pulses. Foods that have a high-GI rating include sugary cereals, white bread and white rice.

However, GI does not consider the *amount* of carbohydrate in a food, and this is why the Glycaemic Load (GL) system was developed. To calculate GL you multiply the grams of carbohydrate in an overall serving by the GI, and then divide by 100. A GL of 10 or below is considered low; 20 or above is considered high.

The list of high-GL foods that have the greatest impact on our blood sugar levels includes sweet fizzy drinks, sweets and cakes. Needless to say, most processed foods contain very refined flours and starches with a high GL[28]. There are also some surprises, like bagels, raisins and rice cakes – foods that are perceived as 'healthy'.

So, why are high-GL carbs & sugars so bad for us?

* Many white carbs and white sugars have been stripped of their natural nutrients, such as trace minerals,

vitamins and antioxidants. Lacking key micronutrients that are required in order to digest them, they force the body to compensate by stealing from its existing nutrient stores. This way, over time, you lose your nutritional reserves[29].

* Blood glucose fuels the brain and rapidly fluctuating blood glucose levels have the potential to diminish concentration and cognitive function[30], which may affect mood[31], behaviour and energy levels.

* We know that the blood glucose 'spikes' that occur after eating high-GL meals slowly damage blood vessels. If this starts during childhood then the damage can accumulate, which may cause cardiovascular and other problems later in life.

* More teenagers than ever before are being diagnosed with type 2 diabetes, a disease which used only to affect older adults. High blood glucose levels from a high-GL diet mean that the pancreas must work harder to produce enough insulin to mobilise glucose out of the bloodstream and into cells around the body. Over time, an overwhelmed pancreas slowly starts to misfire – a state called pre-diabetes – and then eventually stops working altogether, which is when diabetes sets in[32]. Having too much insulin in the bloodstream too much of the time can also affect our ability to metabolise fat; and as a result, more fat is stored, leading to weight gain. Since being overweight, even from the age of 7, can pose a higher risk for type 2 diabetes in adulthood[33], it is good to keep a low-GI mindset.

MODIFIED STARCH – A SUGAR HIT IN DISGUISE

Modified starch is an innocuous-sounding ingredient found in a great number of shop-bought foods, including curries, creamy pasta sauces, yoghurts and tinned rice pudding. It is used as an emulsifier, stabiliser and thickening agent; it can give foods a longer shelf life and make them look fresh and appealing.

On the face of it, this is a relatively harmless food additive; however, it is a refined and highly processed source of carbohydrate which simply gets broken down in the body as sugar. It has a Glycaemic Index of 100 which is the same as glucose and glucose syrup, so it is very pro-inflammatory.

You may see the words 'modified starch' written on the food label but more and more we are seeing corn, potato and rice starches and flours instead, which are still highly refined and essentially the same. This is one of the reasons I encourage you to make your own sauces – see my *Omega Mayo* (page 131) and *My Super-Healthy Ketchup* (page 135).

HOW MUCH IS TOO MUCH?

The government now recommends that added sugar, known as 'free' sugar, should be limited to 5% of the energy (calories) you get from your daily food and drink. This equates to a maximum of 30g of sugar for an adult (roughly seven sugar cubes). See below the maximum recommended daily amounts for all ages. It isn't very much. In fact, it is quite scary how quickly a child can consume their daily allowance: a bowl of cereal and a sweetened yoghurt at breakfast can hit their maximum for the day.

	Daily sugar allowance	Sugar cubes (approx.)
Ages 4–6	19g	5
Ages 7–10	24g	6
Age 11+	30g	7

Source: NHS change4life

N.B. There's no specific sugar allowance for the under-4s but the NHS recommend they avoid sugar-sweetened drinks and food with sugar added to it.

Here are examples of the approximate total sugar in common foods and drinks. Some of the sugar is added, and in some it occurs naturally.

	Gram per serving	Sugar cube(s)
Wholemeal bread (2 slices)	4g	1
Tomato ketchup	4g	1
Jam (1 teaspoon)	8g	2
Baked beans (per can)	10g	2½
Fruit yoghurt	16g	4
Orange juice (1 glass/250ml)	20g	5
Fruit muffin	24g	6
Fruit smoothie (250ml)	24g	6
Flavoured water	24g	6
Apple juice (250ml)	24g	6
Cola	28g	7
Strawberry milkshake	48g	12

It is important to remember that sugar occurs naturally in many foods and drinks and to keep this in mind when shopping for the family. Drinks can be some of the worst culprits for hidden sugar. Beware of seemingly 'healthy' juices. The government recommends you limit fruit juice to 150ml a day.

WHICH CARBS SHOULD OUR KIDS EAT?

A low-carb or no-carb diet is not right for most kids. While our bodies can use fats, protein or carbohydrate as fuel, our brains can only use glucose, and this is why some carbohydrate is needed in the diet to keep our brains sharp. The best way to eat a sensible amount of carbs and keep the GL down is to balance a meal with extra protein, healthy fats and fibre. But it is also important to eat good carbs – by which I mean unrefined wholegrains, pulses and vegetables[34]. These 'complex carbs' are broken down more slowly and lead to a more constant release of energy.

Oats

Oats are one of my greatest kitchen champions. A wonderful source of fibre with a slow, sustained energy release, they contain calcium for growing bones and are also full of antioxidants, iron, magnesium and potassium. Gluten-free oats are available for those who are sensitive to gluten.

Wholegrain brown rice

Brown rice is one of the easiest swaps you can make when trying to change your kids' eating habits. Some kids even prefer it for its nutty taste. Wholegrain brown rice has retained its high-fibre outer hull and bran coating, which contain useful proteins, thiamine, calcium, magnesium, fibre and potassium. Brown rice pasta and noodles are now easily available. They can be a little dry, so try adding olive oil or butter to make them more appealing.

Quinoa
Quinoa is a well-known, seed-like super-grain. It is a source of healthy fibre and is naturally gluten-free; it is also packed with protein and is one of the plant-based grains that contains all the essential amino acids needed to keep you and your children healthy.

Buckwheat
Buckwheat behaves like a grain but is a seed in origin; it is naturally gluten-free and high in protein. You can buy it as toasted or plain groats, flakes (similar to oats) and flour. Nutrient-packed, it has a strong, slightly nutty flavour. We use it to make *Brain-Boost Pancakes* (see page 71).

Sweet potato
Sweet potatoes are bright orange root vegetables and are full of vitamin A, which is essential for good eyesight and a healthy gut. They are rich in other micronutrients and have particularly high levels of vitamin C, which helps us absorb iron from our food.

READ THE LABEL

Here is a list of sugars and sugar substitutes that you might find in the foods you buy, and which you should probably seek to avoid. I have included artificial sweeteners on this list, even though they are calorie-free, as they often also stimulate insulin production.

Acesulfame K (acesulfame potassium)
Aspartame
Cane sugar
Caramel
Corn sweetener
Corn syrup
Dextrose
Evaporated cane juice
Fructose
Fructose-glucose syrup
Fruit juice concentrate
Galactose
Glucose
Glucose solids
Glucose-fructose syrup
Glycerine
Golden syrup
Grape concentrate
Hugh–fructose corn syrup
Inverted sugar
Isomalt
Malitol
Maltodextrin
Maltose
Mannitol
Refiner's syrup
Saccharin
Sorbitol
Sucralose
Sucrose
Sugar beet
Sugar cane

SWEET ALTERNATIVES

I am asked every day by parents which sweeteners they should use as alternatives. Below is my list of recommendations. It takes time for children to get used to eating less sugary foods so aim to cut down little by little. Remember they are all still sugar at the end of the day.

Honey
Honey is one of Mother Nature's sweeteners renowned for its health properties. It has a GI of about 50, which is half that of cane sugar[35].

Maple syrup
Tapped from Canadian maple trees in the spring then boiled down to make syrup, you can't get much more natural than maple syrup. Amazingly 39 gallons of sap only makes one gallon of syrup, which is why it is on the pricey side. Maple syrup has a GI of 54, is packed full of minerals and contains up to 20 compounds that have been linked to human health[36]. The darker grades of maple syrup tend to have more antioxidants than the lighter grades.

Coconut sugar
Also derived from tree sap, coconut sugar looks and tastes similar to light muscovado sugar when dried but is a little coarser. It has a lovely caramel taste that works well in crumbles, brownies or hot chocolate. I find that coconut sugar, with a GI of 35, tends to keep children satisfied for longer.

Blackstrap molasses
Blackstrap molasses has a GI of 55 and is also much more nutritious than sugar. Thick, sticky and treacle-like, it is very strong tasting and a little goes a long way. Molasses is brilliant for tired kids who are suffering from low iron stores – stir a teaspoon or two into their porridge or some hot milk. It also works well in cookies, gingerbread and barbeque sauces. See my *Gingerbread Biscuits* on page 184.

Dates
Dates are gloriously sweet and chewy, and have quite a low GI of around 42. Like most natural sweeteners, they are full of nutrients and fibre that will nourish your children. Dates are also delicious stuffed with almond butter or organic cream cheese, and are great to help sweeten banoffee pies and salted caramel sauces. See my *Mini Raspberry Chocolate Cupcakes* on page 183.

Vanilla
Vanilla is the simplest, sugar-free way to give a sweet impression. Indeed, vanilla is such a complex flavour that it took 107 years to develop an artificial version that tastes like real vanilla. Artificial vanillin is now used in almost every shop-bought vanilla-flavoured food product, as it's so much cheaper than the real thing. However, real vanilla is king in our kitchen – try to buy natural vanilla from vanilla beans; this comes in an essence, a powder or as a pod. It can make all the difference to porridge (see page 74) or in my *Overnight Berry Bircher Oats* (page 80) as well as in cakes and smoothies.

Spices

Spices can be warming and comforting and add potent flavour so that less sweetening is needed. Cinnamon, allspice and cardamom are my favourites, with cloves, mace and nutmeg close behind. They also help reduce inflammation and associated oxidative stress[37]. They taste delicious added to apple compotes, porridges and fruit puddings, as well as curries. Cinnamon is particularly important for kids who tend to get sugar spikes or dips after eating, as it may lessen the impact of carbohydrate in overall glycaemic load[38]. See my recipes for *Apple, Cinnamon & Flax Compote* and *Cinnamon Toast* on pages 68 and 81.

HOW TO CURB SUGAR CRAVINGS

✳ **Offer more water.** Sometimes sweet cravings are a sign of dehydration.

✳ **Dilute fruit juices** so the drink is ¼ juice and ¾ water. Choose fresh juices that are not from concentrate and are made with 100% juice with no sugar added.

✳ **Give them naturally sweet vegetables and fruit** – for example, carrots, baby tomatoes, sweet red peppers, apples, pears, mangoes, bananas, satsumas and berries. These are packed full of fibre, which slows down the rate of sugar absorption and helps your child feel full.

✳ **Avoid foods with added sugar or artificial sweeteners** and swap shop-bought snacks for homemade versions made with honey, maple syrup, coconut sugar, vanilla, cinnamon or dried fruit.

✳ **Eliminate low-fat foods.** When the fat is removed from food it is generally replaced with some type of starch to compensate in consistency and taste. This can send your child on the roller-coaster ride of sugar highs and lows. (See more on this on pages 31–34.)

✳ **Add more protein** to each meal and snack – this is especially important at breakfast time. Eggs are a perfect choice first thing in the day (see recipes on pages 84–88). At snack times, try beany dips and hummus, peanut butter or cheese to accompany chopped fruit and vegetables.

✳ **Get your kids active** – going for a walk, a bike ride or a trip to the playground can distract from sugar cravings. Exercise balances blood sugar levels, boosts energy and reduces stress.

✳ **Encourage more sleep** and downtime. When we are sleep-deprived or stressed, our body tends to yearn for a lift in the form of sugar.

CARBS – 5 TIPS TO REMEMBER

Not all sugars or carbohydrates are equal: some load the bloodstream faster than others.

What you eat with carbohydrates affects the sugar uptake.

Be mindful of your child's recommended daily allowance of sugar: it's probably lower than you realise.

Replace high GI carbs and refined sugars with wholegrains and natural sweeteners.

Kids need to drink plenty of water and get enough exercise and sleep to curb sugar cravings.

LITTLE HERO: EMILIA

Emilia came to me, aged 12, following a year in which her immune system was very fragile, resulting in three separate stays in hospital for infections. She had been on numerous antibiotics and this had affected her gut and immune system. She was tired, run down and finding school a real challenge.

When I asked questions about her diet, I discovered that she had a very sweet tooth, which had become progressively worse over the past year. I explained to her and her mother that at breakfast alone Emilia was eating more teaspoons of sugar than her whole daily recommended allowance and that this was probably compromising her immune system.

Emilia was a determined young girl and just wanted to feel well and spend more time at school and with her friends. She agreed to swap her sugary cereal and fruit juice at breakfast for eggs, porridge and fruit. She also ditched her sweet snacks and stuck to oatcakes and hummus, cheese, sliced carrots and olives instead. At her follow up appointment, her energy was back to normal and she had not even had a sniffle since our first meeting. This lovely story shows how fast a child's health can turn around and suggests how simple diet changes can positively affect so many areas of their life.

When children are growing, they need a constant source of protein to help build new cells. Proteins are vital for the development of children's bones, cartilage, ligaments, skin, hair, nails and teeth. They are also essential for making brain hormones called neurotransmitters – the messenger chemicals that allow the brain cells to talk to each other.

However, getting kids to eat enough protein can be quite a challenge. They seem to be drawn to carbohydrates, so when you have a fussy eater on your hands, 9 times out of 10, the starchy and sweet options win over savoury protein-dense alternatives.

Breakfast is the meal which is often the weak spot, with traditional cooked breakfasts having been ditched for croissants, sugary cereals and sugar-laden 'healthy' cereal bars – all of which are likely to cause an elevated glycaemic response after eating. When kids eat a protein-rich breakfast, not only are they less hungry during the morning, but they tend to choose a smaller lunch[39]. There is also some evidence that it may benefit mental and academic performance at school[40]. This is why my pancake, muffin and waffle recipes contain protein-rich ingredients such as eggs, seeds, milk and yoghurt (see pages 71, 77 and 78).

PLANT PROTEIN

When people think of protein sources they usually think of meat, fish, eggs and dairy products. But plants can also be packed with protein. Examples are nuts, seeds and pulses, as well as 'super foods' like quinoa, chia seeds, flaxseeds, bee pollen and goji berries.

It is important to try to introduce plant proteins into your family meals, since they contain higher levels of phytonutrients than meat-based proteins, as well as having a good concentration of healthy fats and fibre. They also provide protective anti-inflammatory polyphenols. When eaten on their own, some plant proteins do not contain all the amino acids we need, but eating a mix of beans and grains such as lentils with brown rice solves this problem.

CHILD-FRIENDLY PROTEIN

Make meat more digestible

Chewing chunks of meat is not much fun for many kids. Some will refuse point-blank even to put a lump of meat in their mouth, others may chew but spit the meat out later. If you want your kids to eat more than just minced meat, try slow-cooking it – see page 145 for my *Pulled Duck* recipe. Once swallowed, meat can sit undigested in the stomach and make children feel like they have eaten a rock. To boost your child's ability to digest meat, try giving them water with a little lemon or lime juice squeezed into it, or a salad dressing made with apple cider vinegar. Lemon or lime juice can also be used in a marinade to break down the meat before cooking or it can be squeezed over the top after cooking.

Soak the bloat out of beans
Soaking beans and pulses overnight (for a minimum of 8 hours) in a bowl of water with a teaspoon of bicarbonate of soda or a splash of apple cider vinegar not only helps to remove the indigestible starches that can cause wind and bloating, but also helps to get rid of lectins that can damage the gut lining and inhibit digestion in some people. Red lentils and yellow and green split peas have lower amounts of lectins and therefore do not need soaking before cooking.

Get clever with nuts and seeds
A good way of making nuts and seeds more digestible is to turn them into flours and butters.

To make nut flour, simply grind the nuts in a coffee grinder or food processor and use them when baking pancakes, muffins and brownies, as well as for a healthy, crunchy coating for nuggets and fish cakes.

You can buy sugar-free nut butters but it is easy to make your own. Simply dry roast or dry fry nuts and whizz them to a paste using a food processor for about 10 minutes. Always store nut butters in the fridge.

Seed butters are a nice alternative to nut butters. These can be made in the same way or bought ready-made. When using chia seeds and flaxseeds, it is best to soak them in cold water beforehand for at least 20 minutes – but preferably overnight. This makes them more digestible and releases a gel-like coating around the seeds, which is rich in omega 3. However if you are using them ground up in baking or blended up in a smoothie then you do not need to pre-soak them.

MY FAVOURITE SOURCES OF PROTEIN

Plant-based
Almonds
Black beans
Buckwheat
Butter beans
Cannellini beans
Cashews
Chia seeds
Chickpeas
Edamame beans
Flageolet beans
Flaxseeds (also known as linseeds)
Goji berries
Green peas
Hazelnuts
Hemp seeds
Lentils
Peanut butter
Pistachios
Pumpkin seeds
Quinoa
Sesame seeds
Sunflower seeds
Tempeh
Tofu
Walnuts
Yellow split peas

Animal-based
Beef
Chicken
Eggs
Fish
Lamb
Liver
Seafood
Turkey
Venison

Dairy-based
Cheese
Whole milk
Full-fat yoghurt
Kefir

HOW TO BOOST THE PROTEIN IN YOUR CHILD'S DIET

✳ Kids love mini versions of foods so try starting with quail's eggs if they won't eat normal eggs.

✳ Omelettes, frittata and egg muffins are good ways of increasing egg intake.

✳ Try making fresh meat stock. This is one of the most digestible and comforting foods you can give your child. Add it to miso soup, noodle soups and risotto. See page 59 for my delicious and nourishing recipe.

✳ Make pancakes and waffles using ground almonds instead of flour.

✳ Give them seeds and nuts with a fruit snack.

✳ Spread some toast with peanut butter, almond butter, an egg or some homemade baked beans (see page 87).

✳ Blend cooked red lentils or white beans into tomato sauces.

✳ Top oatcakes or buckwheat crackers with cottage cheese, cream cheese or hummus as a savoury snack. Opt for seeded oatcakes for an extra protein boost.

✳ Add chia seeds or flaxseeds to porridge or cereal, or buy peanut butter with added chia and flax.

✳ Sprinkle nuts or seeds on to salads.

✳ Fill dates or celery sticks with cream cheese or nut butters.

✳ Make *Raspberry Chia Jam* (see page 191).

✳ Dip fruit in melted chocolate then roll them in seeds and chopped nuts for a sweet but protein-rich snack.

✳ Add cashew nut butter to soups for creamier and more filling results.

✳ Add milk to smoothies and shakes.

LITTLE HERO: STANLEY

Three-year-old Stanley's mum was very worried as he had become an extremely picky eater. He only ate liquid foods such as porridge, tomato soup and, at a push, rice and pasta. His protein intake was virtually non-existent, and he was often very tired and grumpy. When I had a look in his mouth I could see the reason behind this. He had enormous tonsils. No wonder he was so picky – he simply could not swallow anything very large. Whilst we worked on his immune system to reduce the inflammation and infection in his mouth, we found clever ways of getting more protein and nutrition into his diet. We gave him smoothies boosted with nut butters and seeds, and added lentils to his tomato soups. We were also successful with scrambled egg, meatballs and soft white fish. Thankfully, his tonsils have now returned to the right size and his eating is 100% back on track.

For decades, we have been encouraged to follow a low-fat diet. However, modern science is moving towards an entirely opposite view: that the right fats are essential for keeping us in tip-top condition, physically and mentally.

THE IMPORTANCE OF OMEGA 3

This is the fat most needed by the brain and nerve cells, and is essential for your child's brain development. Omega 3 is also vital for eye health, immunity and the heart, and has natural anti-inflammatory properties.

Eating a diet rich in omega 3 during pregnancy can give your baby a great start in life and may prevent asthma and eczema[41]. Studies have shown that when toddlers and young children get plenty of omega 3 it can affect cognition and influence learning[42]. There are also several studies that show a clear benefit for older children who take omega 3 supplements, including better cognitive performance and behaviour[43–4], improved reading[45], better attention and less hyperactivity[46–7], and even better sleep[48].

Does it have to be fishy?

The best-known way to consume omega 3 is by eating lots of oily fish. Ideally, kids should eat some 2 to 3 times every week. This may sound like a lot, but if you know the tricks it really is manageable. You can make *Mackerel Pâté* (see page 180) as a delicious filling for lunchtime sandwiches and kedgeree or fish pie for supper (see pages 123 and 139). Fish cakes and fish pie are great comfort foods usually enjoyed by youngsters and teenagers alike.

But there are plenty of other good sources of omega 3 for those kids who don't like fish. Organic milk[49] and eggs are an easy option, so too are nuts and seeds, such as flaxseeds, hemp seeds, chia seeds and walnuts. For fussy eaters, grind them up and sprinkle them over muesli, porridge, yoghurt or cereal to supercharge a breakfast bowl.

What about mercury?

There is a justifiable worry about heavy metal contamination in fish, which can harm the human brain and the neurological system[50]. The bigger predator fish, such as large tuna, marlin, shark and swordfish, test high in mercury. So, although tinned tuna is often an easy option, please see this as an occasional food for children rather than an everyday one. Smaller fish, such as salmon, trout, herrings, sardines and anchovies, have a lower risk of mercury toxicity and these should be your first choices for your children.

MY FAT CHAMPIONS

Eggs

I call them 'clever eggs' because they are a brilliant source of phospholipids to fuel the brain. Most children thrive on eating plenty of eggs – and, yes, they can eat them every day, as the cholesterol in eggs is no longer considered a nutrient of concern[51]. The protein inside eggs is the highest-quality protein of any food and contains 22 amino acids. This can make your children feel fuller for longer and help them maintain more stable blood-glucose levels.

Healthy oils

Extra-virgin olive oil is one of the healthiest fats we can give our children. It is rich in oleic acid, omega 3 and omega 6 fatty acids, as well as polyphenols, which are good for our gut health. Extra-virgin olive oil tends to be green in colour and has a tangy peppery taste. It is best to choose extra-virgin oil over the more yellow refined olive oil as it contains more important antioxidants and anti-inflammatories. A good tip is to pour a glug of olive oil over pasta, rice or veggies just before serving.

Cold-pressed rapeseed oil is a good option for general cooking. It actually contains more omega 3 than olive oil and has a higher burning point, at about 230°C. To get the most omega 3 out of it, it is best served uncooked, so add it to salad dressings and mayonnaise (see my *Omega Mayo* recipe on page 131). It has a lovely, mellow, child-friendly flavour.

Coconut oil is an important fat for kids, full of goodness both in its raw state *and* when used in cooking. It is one of the very few oils that you can fry with and which still retains its goodness. It can provide germ-busting qualities and I often recommend it topically for fungal or bacterial skin issues[52] and dry skin niggles – slap it on to chapped lips, any itchiness and nappy rash.

When you eat coconut oil, some of it is converted into ketones, which provide a high-strength, alternative source of glucose. Ketones increase blood flow to the brain, they activate proteins needed for brain repair and they provide the fatty building blocks for new brain tissue – all very important if your child is struggling with learning and development. Some kids love coconut oil and will eat it straight off a spoon; others are not fans and find its flavour overpowering. Luckily you can now buy coconut oil with a neutral flavour quite easily from your local health food shop or online – it has all of the goodness but none of the taste or smell.

Seeds

Seeds feature a great deal in my recipes because children love their crunchiness and mild nutty flavour. Flaxseeds and chia seeds are particularly high in omega 3. Sunflower seeds are a must if your child is not an egg or nut eater, as they contain nutrients that the body uses to create, repair and strengthen both brain and nerve cells. 'Sun-butter' is a brilliant alternative to peanut butter and can be used in baking or dressings.

Avocado

Avocados are one of the healthiest foods in the world and contain many healthy fats and lots of wonderful vitamins[53], including bone-friendly vitamin K, folate and vitamin C. If your child thinks they do not like avocado, then remember to tell them that avocados are also known as alligator pears! This mystery, green, wrinkly fruit is in fact a snappy pear-shaped alligator. If they're still not keen then it can be hidden in smoothies (see my *Green Monster Smoothie* recipe on page 95), soups and even chocolate mousses.

Butter

Cholesterol found in butter fat is important for the development of the infant brain and nervous system. This is partly why breast milk is full of cholesterol[54]. And butter also contains vitamins essential to the optimal growth of children. Butter made from the milk and cream of organic and grass-fed cows is much richer in omega 3 than non-organic. The more yellow the butter, the more likely that it is from grass-fed cows.

The key vitamin in butter is vitamin A, important for good eyesight. It is an essential nutrient for supporting any gut-healing programme, as well as playing an important role in the development of the sexual organs. Butter also contains the antioxidant vitamin E, vitamin B12, important for energy, and vitamin K2, which is an essential bone builder and good for strong teeth.

If your child cannot eat butter, then ghee (clarified butter) may be better tolerated, as it has had most of the allergenic proteins removed.

THE BAD BOYS

Unnatural polyunsaturated fats, hydrogenated and trans fats

Polyunsaturated fats (PUFAs) are not bad in themselves – in fact, they can be extremely healthy for many functions in the body. However, there is a stark difference between natural PUFAs – such as those found in cold-pressed vegetable oils, nut, seeds, wholegrains, meat, dairy produce, fish, seafood and eggs – and cheap, processed versions – found in corn, soya or sunflower oils. In their manufacture, these oils are often processed into solid hydrogenated and trans fatty acids (known as trans fats), which can be used instead of butter or other saturated fats.

Commercially made biscuits, doughnuts and muffins, unless specifically made with butter, are usually stuffed full of trans and hydrogenated fats, so look out for the words hydrogenated or partially hydrogenated vegetable fats on the labels. It seems that these altered fats can, in the long term, make levels of bad cholesterol go up and levels of good cholesterol go down[55]. Trans fats, meanwhile, soak up the antioxidants in the body that are needed for cell repair and may affect the membranes of the brain cells[56].

Deep frying

Deep frying is bad for two reasons. Firstly, the vegetable oils used, such as soya and corn oil, are pro-inflammatory[57]. Secondly, the extremely high temperature required for frying damages the polyunsaturated fats in the oils, as well as the essential fatty acids in the food. It is better to grill, bake or poach your food.

If you do need to fry, use saturated fats, such as butter, ghee or coconut oil, or animal fats such as goose or duck fat, as these are stable when heated to high temperatures.

TOP FAT FACTS

Fats are essential; but know which are your friends and which are your enemies.

Keep track of how much omega 3 your children eat: it's vital for healthy development.

Oily fish is the best source for good fats but don't forget eggs, olive oil, sunflower seeds and avocados.

Avoid deep-frying and try not to use cheap, processed cooking oils.

LITTLE HERO: GEORGE

George, aged 9, was at a very academic school and, despite his high intelligence, was falling behind in his year group. As soon as he walked into my clinic I could see dry, bumpy 'chicken skin' on his face, the tell-tale sign of inflammation and a deficiency of omega 3. He had very wiry hair, drank masses of water during the consultation and was quite twitchy and restless. His teachers and mother were very concerned about his concentration and focus, and homework was a battle.

Luckily, he was keen on his food, so asking him to eat lots of salmon and seeds was nice and easy. I also put him on a daily omega 3 supplement. When he came back to see me for his follow up appointment six weeks later, he was a different boy: calm and happy in his skin. He had been put up to the middle set in some subjects and his focus and school performance continued to improve over the months. It was wonderful to see him bloom into a capable young fellow.

THE GOOD STUFF & THE GUT

The physician Hippocrates was famous for saying 'all disease begins in the gut', and in my clinical experience I have found this to be spot on.

Did you know that we share our bodies with over 10,000 microbial species? We each have about 30 trillion bacteria living in our gut, on our tongue, in our respiratory tract, in the urinary tract and on our skin. These bacteria are generally beneficial or harmless. However, when this delicate microbiome goes out of balance, poor health starts to kick in.

The majority of our microbiome's friendly (good) bacteria live in the lower part of our gut, called the colon. The more diverse and plentiful the good bacteria we have, the better our immune system can fight off the harmful ones.

HOW TO KEEP YOUR CHILD'S MICROBIOME IN TIP-TOP CONDITION

 EAT PLENTY OF PLANTS

The greater variety of foods your child eats (raw and cooked), the more diverse and robust their microbiome will be. Children should be eating at least 20 types of plant foods per week, along with prebiotic and probiotic foods and plenty of fibre[58]

Try to eat a variety of:

* *Vegetables:* spinach, kale, broccoli, carrots, potatoes, red cabbage, red onion, garlic, onion, leek, asparagus, Jerusalem artichoke, beetroot, beans, cabbage, Brussels sprouts and sweet potato.

* *Salads:* vary your leaves to include romaine lettuce, lamb's lettuce, chicory and baby spinach. Try yellow, orange and green tomatoes and peppers, as well as red. Avocado, cucumber and radishes.

* *Fruits:* blueberries, cherries, strawberries, blackberries, plums, raspberries, red apples, black grapes, blackcurrants and bananas.

* *Fresh herbs:* parsley, basil, mint, dill and coriander.

* *Nuts and seeds:* flaxseeds (linseeds), chestnuts, hazelnuts, pecans, almonds, cashews, walnuts, pumpkin seeds and sunflower seeds.

* *Legumes:* cannellini beans, butter beans, lentils, chickpeas, kidney beans, black beans, split peas and adzuki beans.

* *Grains:* black and brown rice and oats.

* *Olive oil*

* *Cocoa*

2 TRY TO INCLUDE SOME FERMENTED FOODS

Fermented foods are high in probiotics – a great source of the good bacteria we need to keep the gut healthy. But getting kids to eat them can be a challenge. Older teenagers with more developed palates may like their slightly sour, tangy flavour, but for young children it is best to start them on fermented foods with more subtle flavours. Here are my kid-friendly favourites:

Yoghurt
Choose plain, full-fat, live yoghurt. Just stir in a teaspoon of honey or some chopped fruit if your child needs a little sweetness.

Kefir
This is a bubbly, slightly sour yoghurt-type probiotic drink you can find in the milk aisle of supermarkets or make yourself. It is a great source of beneficial bacteria, healthy yeast strains, protein, amino acids, calcium, magnesium and a wide range of vitamins, including high levels of vitamin B12. Try my *Kefir Two Ways* smoothies (see page 96) for a gut-healthy drink. Kefir is better tolerated by the digestive system than other dairy products, so can work well for those with a dairy sensitivity.

Apple cider vinegar
This is another wonder ingredient. Make sure to buy it 'unfiltered' and with the 'mother'. This makes it look a bit murky but this way it contains the important friendly bacteria[59]. Use it in dressings, or try my *Tahini Bread* (see page 186) or *My Super-Healthy Ketchup* (see page 135).

GET OUTSIDE MORE

Encourage your children to play outdoors with soil and get muddy. This will allow their microbiomes to encounter trillions of microorganisms within the wider ecosystem. Opening a window and allowing fresh air flow within the home has also been shown to increase the diversity of the microbes within a house.

CHEW PROPERLY

If we do not chew our food properly it is much harder work for the rest of our digestive tract to do its job well. Teach your child to slow down and be more mindful of what they are eating – 10 chews per mouthful is a good start.

PRACTISE GOOD ORAL HYGIENE

It is very important to keep your child's mouth clean and healthy. The mouth houses a lot of bacteria and an overgrowth of bad bacteria will result in continuous swallowing of this bad bacteria. Be mindful that sugar residues linger in the mouth and can ferment into bad bacteria.

WHAT DISRUPTS THE GUT AND MICROBIOME?

Overuse of antibiotics
Antibiotics can be life-saving; however, it is best to keep their use to an absolute minimum as they cannot differentiate good bacteria from bad and can

potentially kill the whole lot, causing significant disruption to the microbiome. So if antibiotics are necessary, ensure you seek advice from a practitioner about supplementing your child's diet with probiotics after the course is finished.

Sugar

Diets high in refined sugar have been shown to negatively influence the function of the microbiome as bad bacteria feed off it, allowing them to increase in numbers and strength. Try and stick to foods that use naturally occurring sugars such as whole fruit or honey[60] instead.

Food additives

Artificial sugars[61–2], sulphites in food preservatives[63] and certain emulsifiers[64] and additives[65–6] commonly found in processed food can harmfully impact the microbiome, even when they occur at government-approved levels. Read food labels carefully and try to avoid these as much as possible.

Allergies and food sensitivities

If your child has a food allergy or food sensitivity, such as gluten, dairy, soya or eggs, then consumption of these foods will be harmful to their microbiome and may lead to gut permeability.

Stress and anxiety

Heightened stress is known to have a detrimental effect on gut health, and one thing can lead to the other, creating a vicious circle. If you have a concern for your child's mental wellbeing, always seek advice from a health practitioner.

But we could all do with trying to reduce the stress in our children's lives. When we are busy we sometimes forget that you have to make a special effort to spend quality time with them – cooking, playing a game or sport, reading stories, and openly communicating about any worries or fears they might have.

THE SCOOP ON POOP

Understanding what your child's poo should ideally look and smell like is key to understanding what is going on inside. I tend to discuss this with both parents and their children as it is important for children to know what to look out for too. (N.B. It is essential to seek medical advice if you ever see blood or mucus in your child's stool.)

Poo shape

The ideal poo shape is smooth and soft sausages in 1–3 pieces and preferably should be passed 1–2 times a day.

Poo colour

Ideally poo is a hazelnut brown colour. If you see a pattern of much paler or darker stools this may be a sign that there is trouble in the tummy.

Poo smells

Poo should not smell foul – healthy kids rarely have smelly farts! Most of the time, smells from the gut are simply due to illness or wrong food choices and this passes quite quickly. A longer term bad smell might reveal that something is out of sync in the gut.

TIPS TO SOOTHE A SORE OR CONSTIPATED GUT

Tummy massage
Massaging a child's tummy in a clockwise direction (never anti-clockwise as this goes against the natural direction of gut flow) with some almond or coconut oil can make a difference to a sore tummy. Start at the bottom left of the abdomen and work upwards, across and then down the right-hand side and repeat a few times.

Flaxseeds
Also known as linseeds, these magical shiny yellow or brown seeds are brilliant at helping bunged up kids poo more easily. They are fibre-rich and have mucilage properties when soaked in water or milk, which can help soothe the gut and release the omega 3 fatty acids from within.

Prunes
Prunes have been used historically to help a sluggish bowel. Kids tend to prefer them stoned and soaked as they are soft and taste lovely and sweet. I always buy them ready soaked for speed. See my *Apple, Cinnamon & Flax Compote* on page 68.

Kitchen herbs
Herbal teas are some of the loveliest ways to soothe a gassy tummy – try peppermint, fresh mint or chamomile. Fennel tea is also very soothing and can even be given to tiny babies. Lemon juice and fresh ginger can be added to many different recipes and can be included in juices and hot drinks.

3 TIPS FOR LOOKING AFTER YOUR MICROBIOME

Feed the microbiome with a variety of gut-friendly foods.

Play outside and get dirty!

Follow up after antibiotics with a gut repair plan.

LITTLE HERO: FRANKIE

Frankie, aged 14 months, had never slept longer than 30 minutes in one stretch. He came to see me with his sleep-deprived mum. She had seen her GP and tried several different strategies to no avail. Frankie showed all the signs of gut pain, such as arching of the back and sleeping curled up in a ball. Luckily, he loved his food, so we slowly started adding in meat stocks, bone broths, fennel, turmeric and other gut-friendly herbs, as well as probiotics. Thankfully he is now sleeping well and has a much happier tummy.

HOW FAKE FOODS AFFECT YOUR KIDS

It is increasingly tricky to shop wisely and healthily for your family. The supermarket shelves are filled with shiny, brightly coloured packaging and even the most wholesome-looking labels and boxes can hide all manner of nasties.

Fake foods tend to be those that are ultra-processed, by which I mean foods that have undergone several industrial processes to be turned into a form that would be almost impossible to recreate in your kitchen. These foods include cereals, noodle pots, cakes, biscuits, fizzy sweet drinks, crisps, nuggets and chewing gum, which contain ingredients and additives, such as emulsifiers and preservatives, that are not readily available to the home cook.

Kids love to have a packet of crisps or a chocolate bar from time to time and most kids have a pretty robust system that can cope with them. However, when ultra-processed food becomes a habit and a bag of crisps appears in the lunchbox daily, or a packet of biscuits is finished off on every bus ride home from school, the body can stop being able to cope and can become inflamed[67].

FAKE FOOD FIENDS

MSG

Monosodium glutamate (MSG) is that umami taste that you find in very concentrated foods such as flavourings and sauces. It is a chemical that tells our brain that something tastes lovely, even if it doesn't really. It is that thing that turns a bland food into something irresistible[68].

MSG has understandably had very bad press in the UK. What you probably don't know is that we all naturally produce glutamate, or glutamic acid[69], and many of us eat quite a lot of it every day, as it occurs naturally in foods like Parmesan, tomato paste, anchovies, mushrooms and peas. So how can glutamate be such a fiend?

The problem occurs when abnormally high concentrations of glutamate build up in the brain, either from excess dietary intake or because of a genetic sensitivity. When too much glutamate tips the balance, it can potentially over-stimulate or excite the brain cells, which over time can misfire the signals between nerve cells and play a role in depression[70], anxiety[71] and obsessive compulsive disorder (OCD)[72–4].

While MSG is only added to a few ultra-processed foods now, glutamate has penetrated our food supply in other ways in the form of extracts and 'natural' flavourings. Yeast extract, for instance, used to only be in things like Marmite and stock cubes but now it seems to be added to a whole host of other foods, such as crackers and flavoured crisps.

Children and teenagers are particularly vulnerable to excess glutamate, since their GABA pathway is still under construction. GABA is the little yogi in our brain that helps us feel calm and relaxed and it works in fine balance with glutamate. If the glutamate pathway is stimulated by highly processed, neurotoxic foods and recreational drugs, including cigarettes, caffeine, and alcohol, it may trigger immature, impulsive and risk-taking behaviours[75]. This is why we need to educate our kids to cut back on processed foods high in glutamate and choose GABA-rich foods to help reach a better balance; foods such as spinach, green tea[76], chamomile tea[77] and brown rice[78], as well as fermented foods like yoghurt, kefir, miso soup, sauerkraut and pickles[79].

Artificial flavourings

When artificial flavourings were exposed as being bad for our health, manufacturers made the move to natural flavourings. This sounds good in theory but they often contain exactly the same chemicals as artificial flavourings[80]. As many of these 'natural' flavours and extracts are quite new, we don't know quite yet what effect they might have on our children's health.

Nitrates

Nitrates and nitrites are chemicals that are often added to processed meats like bacon, ham, sausages and hot dogs. They act as preservatives, helping to prevent the growth of harmful bacteria. However, some studies have linked the consumption of processed meat to colorectal cancer, and this appears to be linked to nitrate content[81]. Confusingly, the majority of the nitrates we eat come from vegetables, such as beetroot, lettuce, carrots, green beans, spinach, parsley, cabbage, radishes and celery, which are otherwise healthy[82]. So, are nitrates naughty or nice? This remains a hotly debated subject. Since my kids love eating sausages and bacon from time to time, I have taken the middle ground and allow them in moderation. I do, however, try to source nitrate-free versions of these meats where possible.

Pesticides

Over 600 unique chemicals make up the 20,000 commercial pesticides used in food production these days. Where pesticides are used, they leave some residue, however carefully the food is washed. Children are more likely to be affected by pesticide residues than adults[83] and studies have shown that they are associated with a broad range of issues, including early puberty[84], neurodevelopmental issues[85], learning difficulties[86] and diabetes[87].

Residue concentrations and risks will vary, but the best way to ensure your child isn't consuming pesticide residue is to go organic, or try and buy local and know where and how your food was grown or produced (e.g. sourcing free-range, grass-fed meat, if possible).

As for vegetables, beware of the 'dirty dozen' – 12 soft fruits and vegetables (where you eat the skin) which have significant levels of pesticide residues. These should be sourced organically

or washed according to the instructions below. Those with tough skins that you remove such as avocado and pineapple and some greens like broccoli and cabbage have much lower levels of pesticides.

THE DIRTY DOZEN 2018

1. Strawberries
2. Spinach
3. Nectarines
4. Apples
5. Grapes
6. Peaches
7. Cherries
8. Pears
9. Tomatoes
10. Celery
11. Potatoes
12. Sweet peppers

Source: www.ewg.org

HOW TO CLEAN VEGETABLES

✳ If organic is not an option, then a good way to wash off some of the pesticide residue is to soak the fruit or vegetables in a large 1–2 litre bowl of water with 1–2 heaped teaspoons of bicarbonate of soda (also known as baking soda) for 5–10 minutes.

✳ Some people use vinegar – I would recommend a splash of apple cider vinegar in the water as it also gives the fruit a lovely shine.

✳ Always rinse the fruit with clean water after soaking.

Artificial sweeteners

Artificial sweeteners are potentially more detrimental for children than sugar. Even though they are officially sugar-free and calorie-free, preliminary research is suggesting that they can stimulate insulin production just as much as sugar[88]. These fake sugars can make you crave sugary snacks and even make those snacks seem less satisfying[89], resulting in increased calorie intake. You can only imagine what influence this has on a child's metabolism in the longer term.

Since the recent UK introduction of a sugar tax, many soft drinks in the UK have had their sugar content reduced. In most cases, however, the sugar has been replaced with artificial sweeteners. You won't be surprised to hear that I suggest avoiding these!

Three artificial sweeteners to avoid:

✳ *Aspartame (E951)* This common sweetener is 200 times sweeter than sugar and despite studies showing it is safe[90], it remains linked to health problems such as an increased risk of cancers and brain tumours[91], as well as early onset puberty in girls[92]. Aspartic acid in excess may possibly overexcite brain cells in a similar way to glutamate[93–4]. Look out for aspartame in fizzy drinks, cordials, low-sugar sweets, diet yoghurts, chewable multivitamins and chewing gum.

✳ *Acesulfame K (E950)* Like aspartame, 'Ace-K' is 200 times sweeter than sugar. There is very little research on the effect of this sweetener on children, so we don't know whether it is inert or a problem for our kids. However, in mice trials, Ace-K contributed to a disturbed gut microbiome and weight gain[95] and impaired cognitive memory functions[96]. Look out for it in cordials and juices, jellies, sweets, yoghurts and chewing gum.

✳ *Sucralose (E955)* This contains zero calories and is up to 650% sweeter than sugar. You can buy it in the sugar section in your supermarket to add to coffee and tea. It is often blended with acesulfame-K. Look out for sucralose lurking in low-sugar and low-calorie fruit juices and cordials, jellies, yoghurts, probiotic drinks, frozen goods, biscuits and chewing gum. It is thought to disrupt the gut microbiome[97].

ANTI-INFLAMMATORY TURMERIC

The best way to reduce inflammation is to adopt a healthy diet low in processed foods containing the fake stuff and refined sugars. But if there's one ingredient that really packs a punch all on its own, it is turmeric. This bright yellow Indian spice has been shown in many studies to have an anti-inflammatory effect. Add it to your child's food in curries and kedgeree (see page 123); another good way to use it is in *Bedtime Turmeric Milk* (see page 103).

LITTLE HERO: TOMMY

Tommy presented with significant challenges associated with his behaviour and socialisation. His mum had cleverly worked out that he responded better on a diet high in proteins and fats with only limited natural sugars. But, while his behaviour and development had progressed well with these diet changes, he had then plateaued, so we decided to dig deeper and run some further laboratory tests.

The main thing these highlighted was extremely high glutamic acid, so we focused on reducing his exposure to any foods high in glutamate. This had an almost instant impact on his mood and behaviour. With a good diet, free from any processed foods and high in GABA-rich foods, such as chamomile tea, he made great gains. He is now at mainstream school and doing brilliantly academically. No one would recognise him as the same boy.

TOO SKINNY, TOO FAT? HOW TO FIND A HEALTHY BALANCE

In my clinic we often see children who struggle to eat enough and to absorb their nutrients, as well as older kids and teenagers who are suffering from depression and anxiety, or from poor body image, and have started restricting their diet in an unhealthy way – if you are worried about a child showing signs of an eating disorder you should always seek professional guidance.

However, the tide is turning, and we are seeing more and more kids who are piling on the pounds faster than they should. This subject is extremely sensitive and complex, and as much as I'd love to clear up the issues around what a 'normal' weight is for kids, the short answer is that there isn't one. Even for adults, BMI has big limitations. And for kids, with all the growth and hormonal changes that are going on and because it is not possible to differentiate between fat and muscle, it is very difficult to use BMI meaningfully.

Kids' short- and long-term health is compromised when they are obese, though, so keeping them at a healthy weight has to be a priority[98]. Many parents are apparently in denial about their children's weight, probably because more children are becoming heavier at a younger age, so we've become used to seeing bigger children[99].

But if you are concerned that your child is getting larger, if type 2 diabetes is in the family, if your youngster is becoming self-conscious, then something needs to change.

Most people still think that being overweight is about eating too much and not being sufficiently active. And it is true that many kids graze all day, hooked on snacks and sweet drinks, and, with only one PE lesson timetabled into a school week, they are simply not getting enough exercise. However, there are other important factors that can contribute to weight gain. Many experts suspect one cause is kids eating too much ultra-processed food[100] and refined sugar. Other causes cited are not enough sleep, as well as stress and anxiety; when this state of mind goes on for a longtime, kids can put on weight.

More and more research is revealing a link between poor gut health and weight gain[101–3]. So a diet that supports the growth of good bacteria in our intestines is vital. One of these is called akkermansia[104], which can help with glucose tolerance[105] and ultimately weight control[106]. Akkermansia levels can be boosted by positive diet changes, such as increasing polyphenol-rich foods like brightly coloured fruit and vegetables[107].

TEN TIPS TO HELP YOUR CHILD LOSE WEIGHT HEALTHILY

1 LEAD BY EXAMPLE

If you eat healthily as a family then your child will be more likely to follow suit.

2 ENCOURAGE CHILDREN TO EAT A RAINBOW EVERY DAY

Have a colour chart on the fridge and get your kids to tick off which fruits and veggies they have eaten that day – purple for blueberries, red for raspberries...

3 DON'T LET THEM DRINK SUGAR

Stick to milk or water at meal times and water in between meals. Or try my fruity water ideas on page 98.

4 CUT DOWN ON WHITE CARBOHYDRATES

White flour and refined grains cause havoc with kids' metabolism – rein in bread, cereals, pasta, pastries, biscuits and cakes.

5 MOVE MORE, EVERY DAY

Children should be active for 60 minutes a day. This can be walking, biking or scooting back and forth from school, or just putting some music on at home to have a dance.

6 KEEP TO CHILD-SIZED PORTIONS

Don't overfill the plate. Use smaller plates if necessary.

7 CUT BACK ON SNACKS AND LATE-NIGHT EATING

They contain dangerous 'hidden' extra calories and research has found that eating late and in-between meals can affect blood sugars and alter metabolism.

8 DON'T USE FOOD AS A REWARD

Think about non-food rewards instead – a sticker, a football card, or a trip to the playground.

9 BE MINDFUL

Mindfulness is one of the most important things that you can teach your overweight child[108] – to help them eat more slowly, control the impulse to overeat and learn to differentiate between eating from boredom and eating because they are hungry. Start by having a no-screens policy at mealtimes.

10 ENSURE ENOUGH SLEEP

Establish a good bedtime routine. It is thought that poor sleep patterns may be linked to poor glucose metabolism and weight gain[109].

BULKING UP YOUR SKINNY BEAN

Having a super skinny child is perhaps less common, but it's just as worrying for parents and equally important to get right. In my clinic I have observed many young children who have poor appetites or are extremely fussy and only eat a handful of different foods.

I also find small or slight children who struggle to grow, despite a good appetite, often have undetected coeliac disease, malabsorption of nutrients or gut inflammation. This means they struggle to extract all the goodness out of the food they eat and it is wise to get them checked out by a professional.

For more straightforward cases here are some tips to get the maximum out of the food they do eat to help them grow and become more robust.

✳ **Hide goodness in drinks.** Include a glass of 100% fruit juice, a Good Stuff smoothie (see page 95) or full-fat milk with every meal.

✳ **Add healthy fats and proteins.** Use ground nuts, seeds, oily fish and dark meat poultry instead of white.

✳ **Use finer foods.** Small grains like couscous, quinoa and angel hair pasta have less air in between, so you will get more of it on their plates.

✳ **Use fat to cook.** Sauté vegetables in lots of olive or coconut oil, butter or ghee.

✳ **Choose higher-calorie veg.** Starchy veggies such as sweet potatoes or butternut squash are more calorie-dense than leafy greens. These can be added to mashed potato, soups or made into fritters.

✳ **Try coconut and nut yoghurts.** These are high in calories and nutrients and can help to increase fat intake.

LITTLE HERO: JIM

Jim, aged 7, had an insatiable appetite. He would eat 5 or 6 large sausages with a couple of eggs at breakfast, a huge school lunch and sometimes 3 chicken breasts with potatoes and veg at dinner. He also loved chocolate and snacks. What was strange was that he was not growing and was very underweight. He also had a terrible memory, was struggling at school and was tired all the time.

When he came to see me, I ran lots of blood tests and a stool test. It turned out that he had some mild gut inflammation and was low in lactobacillus, an important bacteria for making acetylcholine to support memory. Jim literally had a starving body and brain. We put together dietary and supplement strategies to boost his gut bacteria and reduce the inflammation, including turmeric and lots of vegetables. His appetite calmed, and he is now happy and thriving.

TURNING FUSSY EATERS INTO FANTASTIC FOODIES

All sorts of things can cause picky eating in children. And most children will grow out of it on their own. However, restricted or fussy eating needs to be addressed. Even a temporary period of selective eating can have an impact on a child's wellbeing. If poor eating habits go on for a long time, a child can become drained of vital nutrients such as zinc and iron[110–11]. Picky eaters often struggle to sleep through the night[112], which can make the whole household sleep-deprived, run down and more prone to illness. So, the earlier you can encourage and establish good habits the better.

As older children become increasing independent, parents are inevitably less on top of what they eat and when they eat. And this is a time when many teenagers start to skip whole meals and are tempted to snack from vending machines and corner shops instead. Older kids' eating habits can be hugely influenced by their surroundings, including their parents' diet, so your approach to food and showing them good habits during this time, is vitally important.

TIPS TO GET KIDS TO EAT WELL AT MEALTIMES

Cut down on snacks

Snacks can be helpful for keeping mood and energy on an even keel between meals but remember a snack should be a snack, not a mini-meal. Many kids are now eating so many large snacks during the day that they are simply not hungry when it comes to meal times. One oatcake with hummus or half an apple dipped in nut butter is enough to satisfy most young children. You should also avoid fruit juice or cordials in between meals as these can curb their appetite. Stick to water as much as you can.

Watch out for tiredness

Overtiredness is often the reason why children go off their food or are fussy eaters from time to time. Look for underlying reasons for tiredness – perhaps they're having a meal too late, or not getting enough sleep, or attending too many after-school clubs.

Get them more active

Exercise is crucial for fuelling appetite. Take your picky eater to the park or encourage them to play in the garden for an hour before a meal to help them let off steam and work up an appetite.

Be mindful of portion size

Are your eyes bigger than their tummies? Too much food on a plate can be overwhelming for a fussy eater. A great way to work out how much food to give your child at each meal is to look at the size of their palms. One palm-full should equal one portion of each food group (think one for protein, one for carbs and then one or two for veg).

Make it tempting

Would you eat what you are serving your children? If it does not taste good to you, then it probably won't taste good to them either. The better the quality of the underlying ingredients, the tastier they tend to be. Always begin and end a meal with a favourite and known food that they love.

Be persistent

This is a big one. Never stop serving a specific food just because your child refuses to eat it the first time round. And don't make a big deal of any refusal. Put the food on their plate regularly and one day they might surprise you, especially if it looks different, or comes with a sauce you know they love. Sometimes you need to present a food 20 times to a child before they will agree to try it.

If possible, give your children the opportunity to try something new every day. This does not need to be restricted to mealtimes. Give them a little taste whilst you are cooking. One easy strategy is to leave new foods and leftovers on the table in between meals. Your youngster may be curious and have a nibble whilst you aren't looking. Getting them just to pick up a new food is an important first step; be happy if they smell it or place it close to their lips; and, remember, chewing and swallowing a whole mouthful is a huge achievement.

Think texture

In my experience the main reason kids don't like a food is because of the texture rather than the taste of it. Presentation is key here. Try cooking the food in a different way – this may be as simple as how long you steam a vegetable. Crunchy and *al dente* is healthier if they will eat it, but try mushy and soft if they won't. They may love uncooked frozen peas, while cooked or puréed may be a real no-no.

If your child expresses dislike of a food, ask: 'Would you prefer this if it were crunchier/softer?' This allows the child to pin their dislike to the texture, rather the food itself. Then, when you try it next time, remind them that they chose to have it like this.

Lead by example

If there are foods you don't like, don't talk negatively about them, even if you don't eat them. See if you can reframe your approach to food and diet with a more optimistic attitude: 'I can cook with my children to show them what fun and yummy things they can make' or simply, 'I love trying new foods and I'm sure my children will, too.'

Give children choice

Research shows that giving children a few different vegetables with a meal and letting them choose what they eat increases the variety of foods eaten and overall consumption[113]. If you are having trouble, don't just plonk a full plate down in front of them.

Talk and teach

Children naturally want to learn and soak up new information, so talk to them about food and where it comes from. Get them to smell the fresh fruit and veg. Explain simple nutritional principles to allow children to make informed choices.

Frame your words

The words you use when you talk to your children about food are just as important as the food itself. Focus your language on positivity. Load your questions so they can't say no. Instead of saying, 'Did you like the cabbage?' say, 'You tried the cabbage, how was it?' or 'Did you prefer the cabbage or the kale?'

If at first you don't get a positive response, ask them in a different way. Very importantly, though, try not to label a fussy eater. It gives them a perfect excuse to play up to that role.

Have fun in the kitchen and cook together

I am pretty sure the main reason my kids enjoy eating a wide variety of healthy foods is because I have involved them in the cooking process from day one. They love to de-stalk strawberries, peel carrots and mash potatoes. The older ones are now capable of cooking full meals for the family.

For young ones, present food in a fun way – cut fruit into smiley faces, slice sandwiches into mini shapes.

Grow your own food

Gardening with your kids is a wonderful experience. If they can see the food cycle from seed to table, they will be much more willing to try different foods. Even if you only have a tiny garden, balcony or windowsill, think about starting to grow your own herbs and maybe later some vegetables.

Trust your instincts

If you suspect that your child's picky eating is not just a habitual or behavioural issue and may have a more serious cause, then trust your instincts and seek professional advice.

HOW LONG SHOULD A MEAL LAST?

A child's brain will usually tell their tummy that they are full 20–30 minutes after starting a meal. If you try and drag out a meal longer than this, it will be more difficult to get them to finish their plate.

With slow eaters, you need to be hyper-organised with every meal and have everything ready and waiting to be served BEFORE you call them to the table. Maximise that 20–30-minute time slot by ensuring that there are no distractions lurking on the table, such as toys or your mobile phone. Give your child 100% of your attention, so that they eat as efficiently as possible. It can be helpful to have a timer set for 25 minutes, so that you both get used to the time needed for each meal.

Above all, try and stay calm. It makes all the difference.

TOP TIPS FOR HELPING YOUR FUSSY EATER

Manage snacks to ensure your kids have the right appetite at the right time.

Increase activity before meals to build hunger.

Don't load too much on the plate.

Give your kids choices of nutritious new things and be persistent.

Give them your full attention while they are sitting at table.

Keep mealtimes short and stress-free and take food away if it isn't finished.

Above all, lead by example.

LITTLE HERO: EMILY

Emily was 3 when she first came to see me. At that point, she ate just 2 foods: strawberry yoghurt and dry crackers. I noticed that Emily was not making much eye contact or responding to her name and was not yet able to speak a single word. She was prone to recurrent ear infections and colds, she also had very sluggish bowels and a poor appetite. She could not tolerate the noise of vacuum cleaners, the muscles on her legs were very weak, and her days were filled with anxiety and meltdowns.

I have found that gluten and dairy sensitivities are often part of the picture in these situations and I strongly suspected Emily had issues with these foods. Whilst we were waiting for test results, which would confirm the diagnosis, her parents decided to try a gluten- and dairy-free diet anyway. To start with, they swapped the crackers for gluten-free versions and switched the yoghurt to dairy-free. Within weeks, Emily's appetite improved so remarkably that she was eating 3 proper meals per day. She also began speaking! The temper tantrums lessened as she became healthier and she has had no recurrence of the ear infections that had plagued her all her life. She is now a strong and happy young girl with lots of friends and is doing very well at her mainstream primary school.

EATING HEALTHILY WITH ALLERGIES & FOOD INTOLERANCES

Food allergies now affect almost one in ten children and the number is rising. Sneezing, itching, rashes, wheezing, sore tummies and even behavioural issues are common signs of allergies as well as food sensitivities. And if you suspect your child may be allergic to something, it is important to get them checked out as soon as possible. Most allergies can be diagnosed by a simple skin or blood test, while for others it may be a longer process of trial and error – eliminating particular foods and watching for any change or reaction.

An allergy usually appears in the first two years of life[114] – the most common are cow's milk, soya, egg and wheat allergies – and, fortunately, after a few years and a period of dietary exclusion, a child usually grows out of these. However, fish, shellfish, peanut and tree nut allergies tend to be life-long and rarely resolve themselves.

So how to manage it? Removing allergens can be a daunting and difficult task. It can dominate or sway how the entire family eats and organises life; it can be a burden on the family finances as shop-bought free-froms are usually expensive; an allergic child may feel left out at birthday parties and is often forgotten when being catered for on school trips or sports events; and, of course, there is the constant underlying fear of allergen exposure.

Various theories have attempted to explain the rise in food allergies and other atopic diseases, such as eczema and asthma, over the last three decades. Since kids brought up on farms are less likely to develop asthma and allergies[115] and there is a link between vitamin D deficiency and allergies[116], I suspect that fresh air, mud and sunshine play a role in the prevention of allergies.

In many cases of eczema, I have also made the connection between skin health and gut health. It seems that being itchy on the outside is often triggered from also being 'itchy' on the inside and can be accompanied by low-grade gut issues, due to a depleted microbiome.

THE LOW-DOWN ON DAIRY

The most common food allergy, affecting 2–5% of babies, is cow's milk protein allergy (CMPA). Children can also suffer from lactose intolerance, which is when they do not produce enough of the enzyme lactase that helps them digest lactose – the sugary part of milk. CMPA is more likely in early childhood, whereas lactose intolerance usually starts later, from three to four years of age.

The first question every parent asks when their child needs to go dairy-free is, 'How will they get enough calcium?' A child's minimum daily intake of calcium should be 350–550mg for a younger child and 800–1000mg for adolescents. Luckily infant formulas and some dairy-free milks are fortified with calcium. And it is possible to get plenty of calcium from non-dairy foods such as oats, almonds, tinned oily fish, chia seeds, sesame seeds, sunflower seeds, kale, eggs, beef, peas, broccoli, carrots and even some dried fruits, such as apricots, raisins, dried plums and dried pears.

N.B. Some kids seem to have better digestion when they consume goats' milk[117], but it is not an appropriate alternative if your child has an allergy to cow's milk.

Other concerns are:

✳ ***Iodine*** Even mild iodine deficiency can affect school performance and work capacity and it is thought that IQ can be reduced by 7 to 10 points when an iodine deficiency is present[118]. The main dietary sources of iodine, apart from milk and milk products, are fish, shellfish and seaweed. Strawberries, cranberries and potatoes are also good dietary sources, so these are important to include if your child needs to go dairy-free.

✳ ***Protein*** Some dairy-free milks do not contain very high levels of protein. Many almond milks, for instance, only contain about 2% almonds. You will therefore need to think of other sources of protein for a dairy-free child, such as nuts, seeds, meat, eggs, fish and pulses.

✳ ***Vitamin D*** One cup of whole milk contains about 124iu of vitamin D, which your child will miss out on if they go dairy-free. The best source of vitamin D is sunlight in the summer months, so getting outdoors for at least 20 minutes each summer day is helpful for a dairy-free child. (It is important to avoid over-use of sunscreen, too, since it can block the production of vitamin D.) Non-dairy food sources of vitamin D include egg yolks, liver, mushrooms, (particularly shiitake) and oily fish, such as sardines, mackerel and salmon. Some fortified milk alternatives also contain vitamin D. Use rosemary and sage in your cooking as these help in the uptake of vitamin D. Supplementation is recommended during the winter.

HOW TO BE EGG-FREE AND HEALTHY

I suspect one of the hardest dietary restrictions is going completely egg-free, as eggs are one of the single most nutritious foods we can eat and they crop up in almost everything. Egg-free baking is a challenge and I have done my best to make clever swaps in almost all **my recipes.**

Here are some easy ways to stay egg-free and well-nourished:

✳ The **lecithin in eggs**, which is an important brain food, can be replaced by lecithin from sunflower seeds.

* **The vitamin A** you would normally get from eggs can be obtained from butter, full-fat hard cheese, sweet potato, carrots, squash, red peppers, dark leafy greens, peas, dried apricots, cantaloupe melon, mango, peaches and papaya, as well as one of my favourite spices, paprika.

* To replace the **fat-soluble vitamin D** in eggs, you could use butter or full-fat hard cheese (see other vitamin D food sources above, like sunlight).

* There is **folic acid** in eggs, but alternative sources are green leaves like kale, spinach, brussels sprouts and cabbage, as well as pak choi, cauliflower, asparagus, beetroot, leeks, okra, parsley and parsnips.

* **Vitamin B12** is needed to make red blood cells. If levels are insufficient, the nervous system can become damaged. To replace the vitamin B12 in eggs, you can use other animal sources, such as meat, fish, seafood or cheese, or else take a good-quality supplement. Marmite and other yeast extracts contain B12.

* Eggs provide **iron**, which the blood needs to carry oxygen around the body, but this can also be obtained from meat, beans, lentils and spring greens. It is best to eat vegan sources of iron with vegetables or fruit, as vitamin C increases its absorption.

How to replace eggs in baking

The alternatives listed here are particularly good swaps for egg when making pancakes, muffins, cakes and waffles; however, they do not work at all for quiches or other very obviously eggy dishes. I do find that if the recipe calls for more than 2 or 3 eggs then it is best to use a combination of the options below. To swap a recipe that demands 4 eggs, for example, I suggest: 2 flax eggs (see recipe below) and ½ cup apple purée or 2 chia eggs and 1 banana. You can also use specialist egg-replacer mixes from health food shops.

Each option can be equivalent to 1 egg:

* Flax egg: 1 tbsp (7g) ground flaxseeds mixed with 2½ tbsps (40ml) water

* Chia egg: 1 tbsp (7g) ground white chia seeds mixed with 2½ tbsp (40ml) water

* ½ banana mashed

* 2 tbsp arrowroot combined with 3 tbsp water

* 1 tbsp peanut butter, cashew nut butter or almond butter

* ¼ cup (50g) apple purée

* 2 tbsp baking powder mixed with 2 tbsp water and 1 tbsp oil

ALL ABOUT GLUTEN

Gluten is the sticky stuff in flour that helps bind bread, pasta and cakes. It is present in wheat, rye, barley and some oats.

Some children can have a marked allergy or sensitivity to wheat and/or gluten but the main health issue linked to eating gluten itself is coeliac disease. This is an auto-immune response to eating gluten where our immune system fights the villi in our small intestine and this stops proper absorption of nutrients from our food into our bloodstream. It seems to affect 1 in 100 Europeans and the only known treatment for coeliac disease is life-long avoidance of gluten. Even one tiny exposure can trigger a violent reaction, which makes managing coeliac disease very hard.

Ninety-five per cent of those with coeliac disease have inherited a genetic predisposition, similarly, gluten can be part of the progression of other autoimmune diseases such as type 1 diabetes[119], rheumatoid arthritis[120] and autoimmune thyroid conditions[121]. So if you have coeliac disease or autoimmunity in the family it may be worth getting this checked out if you suspect gluten is an issue.

Going gluten-free is much easier than it once was, with supermarket aisles bursting with gluten-free products. But a word of caution. Gluten-free breads and cookies are usually highly processed, sugary and tasteless, so you might want to consider baking your own or only buying these occasionally. My *Tahini Bread* on page 186 is a winner on the taste front and is a doddle to bake. Those who have to follow a gluten-free diet also need to ensure they are getting enough B vitamins, iron and dietary fibre. Luckily meat, eggs, black beans, molasses and leafy greens provide most of these.

LITTLE HERO: MOLLY

Molly developed eczema from an early age and certain foods seemed to cause it to flare up and trigger gut issues. Her mum sought advice from a paediatrician, who ruled out the common allergies and coeliac disease. However, her skin was still reacting and her poo was usually too soft. Through a process of elimination, her mum and I worked out that her skin and gut were affected by many foods, including wheat, egg white, cows' milk and even the humble pea! I suggested Molly avoid all these foods, and that she combine this regime with some probiotics. Her skin and gut cleared up within a couple of weeks. We are now hoping to add back baked eggs and cooked cow's milk gradually, as this would make a huge difference to her life and her underlying nutrition.

MY FIRST AID TOOL KIT

Having a child who is ill is one of the most upsetting parts of being a parent. So here I share Mother Nature's best immunity boosters. You can use these tips regularly to prevent snuffles and sneezes, especially during the winter months. Or, if an illness comes on suddenly, you may find some of them helpful at knocking things on the head faster.

Chicken soup, stock or broth
A traditional cold and cough buster[122] and one the most immune-friendly foods there is. Here are instructions on how to make the perfect chicken stock:

1 chicken carcass
1 carrot, chopped into 3 pieces
1 stick celery, halved
1 onion, halved, retaining the skin
1 bay leaf
1 sprig of parsley
1 sprig of thyme
8 peppercorns
1 tbsp apple cider vinegar or lemon juice
2 litres filtered water

Preheat the oven to a 200°C /gas mark 4.

Place the carcass into a large ovenproof dish and cook it in the oven for 20–30 minutes to brown the bones.

Remove the dish from the oven and place it on the hob over a high heat. Add the carrot, celery, onion, herbs, peppercorns and apple cider vinegar or lemon juice and at least 2 litres of filtered water. Bring the liquid to a boil, cover, then turn down the heat to a slow simmer, or return the dish to the oven at 110°C/gas mark 2 for at least 6 hours. Skim off any scum from the top of the liquid as it cooks.

Remove from the heat and strain the liquid through a sieve, discarding the vegetables and bones. Leave it to cool completely.

Store in the fridge if using that week or in the freezer in soup bags or ice lolly/ jelly moulds.

Oranges and lemons
Citrus fruits are a great source of vitamin C, which is vital for immunity. Other good sources are strawberries, kiwi fruit, pineapple, red peppers, parsley, kale and raw cacao.

Fresh ginger
Ginger is one of nature's wonder foods, full of nutrients, antioxidants and vitamins, with antibacterial properties[123]. It is one of the first ports of call when illness strikes our household. Simply juice a small piece of peeled fresh ginger (the size of your child's thumb) with a couple of apples, then get your kids to down the shot in

one. You may want to 'chase' the shot with more apple juice, but most kids love the ginger kick. If you do not think your kids are quite up for that yet, then try my *Zingy Carrot Juice* on page 102 or some delicious *Chinese Ginger Chicken with Brown Noodles* on page 136.

Garlic

Garlic is a super ingredient that will not only pack that extra punch of flavour but will also boost your immune system[124]. Add extra garlic to your cooking, particularly over the winter months, to benefit from its vast number of immune-boosting properties.

Honey

Honey is well known for its medicinal and antibacterial properties[125]. We always have honey in our cupboard and it is one of the first things I turn to if anyone is ill. Remember not to give a baby any honey until they are over 12 months old – this is because of the risk of being infected with *clostridium botulinum*, which can cause infant botulism (a rare condition that attacks the nervous system and causes paralysis).

Elderberry syrup

Dark purple elderberries are packed full of antioxidants, flavonoids and vitamins[126], and act as an anti-viral. Elderberry, specifically, helps to treat the dreaded flu virus[127]. It may also help to reduce the duration of the common cold[128] – I give this to my kids when they are coming down with a sniffle or a sneeze.

You can now easily buy elderberry syrup in your local health food shops. Better still, go in search of elderberries in the hedgerows to make your own[129]. They are conveniently in season pre-winter, in September and October – Mother Nature giving us a helping hand just when we need it. It tastes a bit like blackcurrant cordial and mixes well into a berry smoothie, if your kids are fussy with new tastes. Take 1 to 2 teaspoons up to 4 times a day at the first sign of a virus coming on; or take 1 to 2 teaspoons daily as a healthy tonic to ward off viruses and to boost your child's immune system.

Probiotics

As we have seen, probiotics are of huge importance for gut health. They also have therapeutic potential in preventing and treating several immune-response-related diseases, including viral infections[130]. One of the other great things about probiotics is that they seem to reduce the length of an upper respiratory illness in children[131].

Sunshine

Why is sunshine so important for our health and wellbeing? We need it to synthesise a feel-good nutrient called vitamin D, which is vital for every single cell in our bodies. We also need it for supporting our immune system, as well as ensuring that calcium enters the bones.

A number of foods naturally contain vitamin D, including milk, eggs and oily fish. But we receive the majority of the vitamin D that our bodies need through our skin's exposure to the sun. The lack of sunshine in the UK, particularly in the winter months, is a major factor in why we tend to fall short and this is not helped by our increasingly indoor lifestyle.

Parents tend to slap sun cream on their kids at the first hint of sun and yet it is thought that letting your child have a few minutes of cream-free sun makes all the difference to their vitamin D levels[132].

Public Health England[133] recommends that during the winter months everyone should have a supplement of 10 micrograms of vitamin D daily. If you are concerned that you or your family are not getting enough, the best bet is to get a simple finger prick blood test organised through a practitioner in order to know what level of supplementation is needed, and to be monitored regularly.

THE BOTTOM LINE

By now, you should have gathered that for most people who follow a good diet, vitamin and mineral food supplements should be unnecessary. But some people such as fussy eaters or those on a restricted diet don't get enough naturally. This is where supplements can be useful, including probiotics, vitamin D and fish oils. You can also find my recommendations at www.naturedoc.clinic/thegoodstuff.

LITTLE HERO: CHARLIE

This is a personal little hero story to show the amazing power of what some well-timed nutrient-dense good stuff can do.

There was a nasty virus doing the rounds at my son Charlie's school, knocking children out for two weeks. On top of this, one of the students had developed sepsis and was hospitalised. Of course, all the parents were on high alert. And so when I picked Charlie up from school, and he said he wasn't feeling very well., I thought we would be in for the long haul. He was hot to touch, very quiet, looked pale and had a runny nose and a cough.

I immediately gave him some elderberry syrup, and, since he was not hungry, I also gave him a large *Zingy Carrot Juice* (see page 102) full of ginger, vitamin A and vitamin C. Brilliantly, this seemed to do the trick as when he woke up the next morning he was back to his normal bubbly self.

THE GOOD STUFF

If I had to pick one single piece of advice to help you improve your child's diet, it would be to cook more from scratch. When you know the tricks, home cooking does not need to be time-consuming or expensive. Most of the recipes that follow are either fairly quick to prepare or can be made in advance and stored in the freezer. There are also many recipes that do not involve any cooking at all.

All my recipes have been tried out on my kids, their friends and my nephews and nieces, and they have only been included if they have had a (near) unanimous thumbs up. You will find lots of easy, healthy lunchbox and snack ideas, as this is where parents tend to struggle the most.

Where possible, the recipes also have clever swaps to enable you to make them free of the 14 most common food allergens, and they can be adapted to gluten-free. Most of the ingredients can be found in your local supermarkets and should be easy to include in your weekly shop. There are a few exceptions for some of the specialist allergen-free ingredients so to source these you can refer to our shopping guide at www.naturedoc.clinic/thegoodstuff.

My family loves chocolate, puddings and biscuits and I wouldn't dream of depriving them of this joy – a childhood without sugar could end in mutiny! However, I use natural sweeteners like honey and maple syrup and try to find smart ways to reduce sugar wherever I can: my recipes use less of it than you will find in most other cookbooks or shop-bought treats. If possible, reduce the quantity of sugar by 5–10g every time you cook a sweet recipe. You will be astounded by how little sugar your children actually want or need.

Generally, I have kept to low or no salt; however, sometimes a pinch of sea salt can really bring the taste of a recipe alive, so it is your choice. A good tip is to put the salt in at the end, just before serving, so the tongue can be tricked into thinking there is more salt than there really is.

Feeding your children is one of the most emotionally charged aspects of parenting; and, as a working mum of 3, I know how hard it can be to cook healthy food that kids will actually eat.

I'm passionate about my cause, but I am also a realist. If my children do now – mostly – choose healthier options, this has not been through cocooning them away or banning pizza, chips and cake. I have never aimed for a perfect diet; I have just done my best to feed them 'the good stuff' most of the time.

CHAPTER ONE

BRILLIANT BREAKFASTS

GRANOLA

A jar of homemade granola is a great standby for speedy breakfasts. Kids love the crunch, especially when mixed with thick Greek yoghurt and topped with homemade compote (see page 68). I have kept this recipe simple with picky eaters in mind, but you can jazz it up by adding raisins, mulberries, chopped apricots, goji berries, coconut flakes, pecans, flaked almonds, chia seeds or flaxseeds into the cooked oat mixture. Store the granola in a large glass jar for up to three months.

MAKES 10 PORTIONS

- 4–5 tbsp runny honey
- 3 tbsp coconut oil (with a neutral flavour)
- 300g rolled oats
- 40g pumpkin seeds
- 40g sunflower seeds

Preheat the oven to 180°C/160°C fan/gas mark 4.

Melt the honey and coconut oil together in a small saucepan over a gentle heat.

Meanwhile, scatter the rolled oats, pumpkin seeds and sunflower seeds over a large baking tray. Pour over the honey mixture and mix to coat well.

Bake in the oven for 20–25 minutes, shaking every 5 minutes so that it browns evenly.

Remove the tray from the oven and leave to cool.

FRUIT COMPOTES

Compotes are delicious and healthy, and go really well with granola, porridge, waffles, pancakes, kefir (see page 96) and even ice cream or cake. Store compote in a glass jar in the fridge for up to a week or freeze in small batches.

MIXED BERRY COMPOTE

You can use fresh berries when they are in season. Frozen berries work just as well in the winter. My family love a combination of raspberries, blackberries, blackcurrants and redcurrants. The purple and red polyphenols in berries help to reduce inflammation and support gut health.

ooooooo

MAKES 6–8 PORTIONS

2 pears, peeled, cored and diced
225g mixed berries
1–3 tbsp coconut sugar or light muscovado sugar

Place a saucepan over a medium heat and cook the pears for 10 minutes, or until they are soft (this part may be skipped if your pears are already very ripe).

Add the berries and cook for about 10 minutes, stirring to break everything down to a mush.

Sweeten to taste with the coconut sugar – the amount will depend on how ripe the fruit is and which berries you use.

For older children you can leave the compote nice and chunky, but for younger ones it's best to serve it smooth, so blitz it with a blender for about 45 seconds.

APPLE, CINNAMON & FLAX COMPOTE

A thick and yummy combination of gut-friendly fruits, seeds and spices. We use eating apples rather than cooking apples for children as they are naturally sweet. Choose any variety except Granny Smith or Golden Delicious. If you serve this compote cold, you will preserve the natural omega 3 in the flaxseeds. Whether cold or warm, you will get all the healthy fibre.

ooooooo

MAKES 6–8 PORTIONS

4 apples, peeled, cored and diced
6–8 soft pitted prunes, cut into small pieces
¼ tsp ground cinnamon
1 heaped tbsp flaxseeds, ground in a food processor or coffee grinder

Place a saucepan over a medium heat, add in the apple, prunes and cinnamon and cook for about 10 minutes, or until the apple is soft.

Blitz the mixture with a hand blender for about 45 seconds until it is smooth.

Allow the fruit to cool before stirring in the ground flaxseeds.

APPLE, CINNAMON & FLAX COMPOTE
MIXED BERRY COMPOTE

BRAIN-BOOST PANCAKES

These are a fun and filling way to start the day or a healthy option for lunchboxes. Buckwheat is a seed rather than a grain and is naturally gluten-free. It's also bursting with magnesium, an important nutrient for the developing brain.

MAKES 12 SMALL PANCAKES

- 120g buckwheat flour
- 140g spelt or wholemeal flour
- ½ tsp fine sea salt
- 1¼ tsp bicarbonate of soda
- 50g coconut sugar or light muscovado sugar
- 4 tbsp butter, melted
- 2 free-range eggs
- 250ml plain Greek yoghurt
- 300ml whole milk
- ½ tsp coconut oil (with a neutral flavour) or butter, for frying
- *Optional extras:* fresh blueberries, raspberries or sliced banana and organic maple syrup

Combine all the dry ingredients in a large bowl and all the wet ingredients in another.

Tip the wet ingredients into the dry and beat together with an electric whisk. Leave the mixture to stand for 5–10 minutes.

Place a non-stick frying pan over a medium to high heat. Lightly coat the pan with coconut oil or butter and pour in enough batter to make a pancake about 10cm in diameter. As soon as the pancake starts to bubble, in about 45–60 seconds, flip it over and cook for 15–30 seconds until it is golden brown on both sides.

Serve the pancakes warm with fresh blueberries, raspberries or sliced banana and maple syrup.

GLUTEN-FREE

Use gluten-free plain flour.

DAIRY-FREE

Use oat, coconut or almond milk, coconut yoghurt and dairy-free spread.

EGG-FREE

Use 2 tbsp ground flaxseeds mixed with 5 tbsp water.

PORRIDGE THREE WAYS

Porridge is a nourishing and satisfying breakfast for hungry children. Supercharging it with extra nutritious goodies can boost its protein and healthy fat content, so your kids are less likely to snack on the sweet stuff mid-morning.

SERVES 2–3 CHILDREN
100g porridge oats
400–500ml whole milk

Add the oats and milk to a saucepan and place over a medium heat and cook for 5–10 minutes, stirring frequently, or until the porridge is nice and thick.

Leave it to cool a little before adding the other ingredients – see page 74 for *Simply Supercharged*, *Hazelnut Choc* and *Berry Nice* ideas to help them feel fuller for longer. Mix everything together well.

Pour the porridge into a bowl, add a little extra milk, if needed, and serve.

DAIRY-FREE
Use your child's preferred dairy-free milk, such as almond, hazelnut, cashew or coconut.

GLUTEN-FREE
Use gluten-free oats.

SIMPLY SUPERCHARGED PORRIDGE

Fussy eaters won't notice the seeds in this but will benefit from the added omega they provide. To prepare a week's worth of omega 3-rich seed mix: combine 2 tbsp sunflower seeds with 2 tsp chia seeds and 2 tsp flaxseeds and grind them in a food processor or coffee grinder to form a fine powder (alternatively, you can use tahini). Store the mixture in a glass jar in the fridge.

ooooooo

SERVES 2–3 CHILDREN
1–2 tsp omega 3-rich seed mix (see above)
1–2 tsp runny honey

HAZELNUT CHOC PORRIDGE

This tastes decadent and is perfect for those who are starting to wean their children off sugar-laden processed cereals. What's more, it's full of health-enhancing polyphenols that support gut and cell health.

ooooooo

SERVES 2–3 CHILDREN
2 heaped tsp raw cacao powder or cocoa powder
¼ tsp vanilla essence
1 tsp coconut oil (with a neutral flavour) or butter
1 tsp hazelnut or cashew nut butter
1–2 tsp maple syrup

BERRY NICE PORRIDGE

Your little ones will love this deliciously sweet bowl of goodness. The magnesium-rich cashew nut butter should help them feel fuller for longer.

ooooooo

SERVES 2–3 CHILDREN
4–8 raspberries
1–2 tsp cashew nut butter
1–2 tsp maple syrup
½ tsp freeze-dried raspberry pieces*

. . . .

*You can find freeze-dried raspberry and strawberry pieces in the baking section of large supermarkets.

SHORTCUT

Use 2–3 heaped tsp *Hazelnut Choc Spread* (see page 190).

SIMPLY SUPERCHARGED PORRIDGE

BERRY NICE PORRIDGE

HAZELNUT CHOC PORRIDGE

BLUEBERRY & BANANA MUFFINS

These little beauties are packed with nutrients that promote brain health. They are light and fluffy with just enough sweetness, so they don't cause a big sugar spike. You may be surprised to see that I use a whole courgette. This sneaky ingredient is a clever way of getting some greens in. You can blitz the sunflower seeds in a blender if you have a fussy eater.

MAKES 18 MUFFINS

- 3 free-range eggs
- 150g coconut sugar or light muscovado sugar
- 1 courgette, grated
- 1 banana, mashed
- 175g spelt or wholemeal flour
- 160g ground almonds
- 2 tsp baking powder
- ½ tsp bicarbonate of soda
- ¼ tsp fine sea salt
- 150g blueberries (fresh or frozen)
- 50g sunflower seeds

Preheat the oven to 180°C/160°C fan/gas mark 4 and line muffin tins with 18 muffin paper cases.

In a large bowl, whisk the eggs and coconut sugar together for 3 minutes using an electric whisk, or until they are nice and creamy.

Add the grated courgette and mashed banana and whisk again briefly.

Add the flour, ground almonds, baking powder, bicarbonate of soda and salt, and mix together with a spatula until well combined.

Finally, fold in the blueberries and sunflower seeds.

Drop a small ice-cream scoopful of muffin mixture into each muffin case then bake in the oven for 25 minutes, or until they have risen and the tops are golden brown.

NUT-FREE

Replace the ground almonds with 160g sunflower seeds ground to a flour in a food processor. No need to add the extra sunflower seeds at the end, in this case.

GLUTEN-FREE

Use rice flour or gluten-free plain flour.

EGG-FREE

Use 3 tbsp ground flaxseeds mixed with 7½ tbsp water.

CARROT & POPPY SEED WAFFLES

Kids love waffles and these are a healthy and tasty alternative to the bland shop-bought varieties. If you have a super-fussy eater, this is one of the recipes I recommend you try first. Bet they won't spot the hidden carrot! As well as giving an extra crunch, the poppy seeds boost calcium, iron and zinc levels.

MAKES 5–6 WAFFLES

200g porridge oats
4 tbsp coconut sugar or light muscovado sugar
1 tsp baking powder
1 tbsp black or white poppy seeds
Pinch of fine sea salt
1 medium carrot, peeled and grated
200ml whole milk
120ml plain Greek yoghurt
3 free-range eggs
Coconut or olive oil, for greasing the waffle maker

Preheat the oven to 180°C/160°C fan/gas mark 4 and lightly grease your waffle iron with a little coconut or olive oil, using a piece of kitchen paper.

Measure the oats into a food processor and blitz for about 1 minute, or until they reach a flour-like consistency.

Transfer the oats to a large bowl and stir in the coconut sugar, baking powder, poppy seeds and salt, before adding the grated carrot, along with the milk and yoghurt.

Add one egg at a time, beating well after each addition until all the ingredients are combined.

Turn your waffle maker to the highest setting and pour a ladleful of the mixture into the lower plate. Be careful not to overfill it or the mixture will come pouring out of the sides. Close the lid and let the waffle cook until it is golden brown on both sides, about 2 minutes.

Remove from the waffle iron and place on a baking tray. At this stage, it will still seem quite soft, so pop it into the oven for 5 minutes to crisp up.

Repeat until you have 5–6 waffles.

EGG-FREE
Use 3 tbsp ground flaxseeds mixed with 7½ tbsp water.

GLUTEN-FREE
Use gluten-free oats and gluten-free baking powder.

DAIRY-FREE
Use oat, coconut or almond milk and coconut yoghurt.

OVERNIGHT BERRY BIRCHER OATS

My nieces always ask for this delicious breakfast when they come to stay. It takes seconds to prepare the night before, or last-minute in the morning – just halve the quantities of milk and yoghurt. Ring the changes by swapping the berries for mango and passionfruit, or more traditional grated apple and cinnamon.

SERVES 3–4 CHILDREN

- 100g porridge oats
- 250ml whole milk
- 150ml plain Greek yoghurt
- 3 tbsp mixed berries (fresh or frozen)
- ½ tsp vanilla essence
- 3 tsp chia seeds
- 1–2 tsp maple syrup

Simply mix all the ingredients together in a bowl before bedtime and pop it in the fridge overnight.

In the morning, give the mixture a quick stir and add some extra berries and yoghurt, if needed.

DAIRY-FREE

Use your child's preferred dairy-free milk and yoghurt. We like almond milk and cashew yoghurt.

GLUTEN-FREE

Use buckwheat, quinoa, millet flakes or gluten-free oats.

CINNAMON TOAST

This is one of the easiest ways to get protein into your child's breakfast. So many parents say that their children won't eat eggs, but I bet they will this way. I sweeten the dish with cinnamon, which also helps to keep blood sugar levels well-balanced and staves off mid-morning hunger pangs.

MAKES 1 SLICE

- Knob of butter or coconut oil (with a neutral flavour), for frying
- 1 free-range egg
- ¼ tsp ground cinnamon
- ¼ tsp vanilla essence
- 1 slice wholemeal seeded or sourdough bread
- Drizzle of maple syrup, to serve

Melt the butter or coconut oil in a large heavy-based frying pan over a medium heat.

Meanwhile, crack the egg into a wide, flat bowl and beat in the cinnamon and vanilla essence with a fork.

Dip the bread into the egg mixture, making sure it is evenly covered.

Fry the bread in the pan for 3–4 minutes on each side, or until it is golden brown.

Remove from the heat and place on a plate.

Drizzle a little maple syrup onto a palate knife and spread it over one side of the toast. Cut it up into soldiers to serve.

EGG-FREE

Blend a banana with the cinnamon and vanilla, add 50ml milk and dip the bread in this mixture before frying.

GLUTEN-FREE

Use gluten-free seeded wholemeal bread.

CRUNCHY BREAKFAST PEBBLES

Kids love cereal but almost every option in the supermarkets is laden with sugar and made with highly-processed grains. These little choccy pebbles contain no refined sugars or flours. They can be eaten dry and crispy as a snack or mixed with milk in a bowl for breakfast.

○○○○○○○

MAKES UP TO 8 BREAKFASTS (IF YOU CAN RESIST THEM AS A SNACK)

4 free-range eggs
50g coconut oil (with a neutral flavour), melted
100g runny honey
1 tbsp vanilla essence
70g (4 heaped tbsp) coconut flour
3 tbsp raw cacao powder or cocoa powder
¼ tsp fine sea salt
¼ tsp bicarbonate of soda
Light oil, for greasing

Preheat the oven to 170°C/150°C fan/gas mark 3 and line two large baking trays with Silpat silicone sheets or greased parchment paper.

Whisk the eggs in a bowl then add the melted coconut oil, honey and vanilla essence and whisk again.

Stir in the coconut flour, cacao or cocoa powder, salt and bicarbonate of soda and mix well.

To make the pebbles, roll ½–1 tsp of the mixture into a small ball and place it on the prepared baking tray. Squash the ball gently with your thumb to make a flat pebble. Repeat with the rest of the mixture. These don't expand much so you only need to leave a small gap between each one.

Bake the pebbles for around 9–11 minutes. Turn all the pebbles over and cook for a further 6–8 minutes. They should be cooked through but still soft to the touch. This may take some practice.

Remove the trays from the oven and transfer the pebbles to a wire rack – they will crisp up as they cool.

Store them in a glass jar for up to a week.

EGG-FREE

Use egg replacer powder or 4 tbsp ground flaxseeds mixed with 10 tbsp water.

GREEN EGG & HAM MUFFINS

These are quick to cook and can be made the night before and reheated. Great for eating on the school run if you are rushed.

MAKES 4 MUFFINS

2 free-range eggs
1 slice prosciutto ham, finely chopped
Handful of baby spinach leaves, finely chopped
1 sprig of parsley, leaves finely chopped
1 tsp mixed Mediterranean herbs
Olive oil, for greasing

Preheat the oven to 180°C/160°C fan/gas mark 4 and grease four holes of a deep muffin tin. Place the tin in the oven to heat up for 1–2 minutes.

Beat the eggs in a bowl then mix with the rest of the ingredients.

Pour the mixture into the greased holes until they are about two-thirds full.

Bake the muffins in the oven for 10–12 minutes, or until they are nice and brown on top.

SMOKY SAUSAGE, EGG & BEANS

A hearty Sunday breakfast or brunch for the whole family, this is also a great fallback for a quick and easy supper. These smoky no-sugar beans are so delicious you will never want to open a tin of baked beans again.

SERVES 4 CHILDREN

- 12 mini cocktail or chipolata sausages
- 1 tbsp olive oil
- 1 large onion, diced
- 2 garlic cloves, diced (optional)
- 2 carrots, peeled and diced
- 2 celery stalks, trimmed and diced
- 2 tbsp tomato concentrate
- 2 tbsp Worcestershire sauce
- 1 tsp smoked paprika
- 2 tbsp fresh parsley, chopped
- 2 x 400g tins chopped tomatoes
- 2 x 240g tins haricot beans
- 8 quail eggs (or 4 free-range chicken eggs)
- Olive oil, for greasing

Preheat the oven to 180°C/160°C fan/gas mark 4 and grease a roasting tin with a little olive oil.

Place the sausages on the baking tray and cook in the oven for 25 minutes, or until they are browned and cooked through. These will be added to the beans later.

Meanwhile, place a large saucepan over a low heat, add the olive oil and fry the onion, garlic, carrots and celery gently for 4–5 minutes, or until soft.

Stir in the tomato concentrate, Worcestershire sauce, smoked paprika and half the parsley, followed by the chopped tomatoes and haricot beans. Increase the heat to medium and cook the mixture uncovered for 30–40 minutes, then pour it into a large roasting tin.

Make holes in the bean mixture with the back of a spoon and crack an egg into each one.

Stick the sausages into the mixture in between the eggs and place the dish in the oven for 10 minutes, or until the eggs have set.

Sprinkle the remaining parsley over the top and serve.

GLUTEN-FREE

Use gluten-free sausages and a gluten-free Worcestershire sauce, such as Biona.

CELERY-FREE

Use fennel instead.

EGG-FREE

Omit the eggs and sprinkle grated Cheddar on top.

EGG & SALMON MINI ROLL-UPS

Full of protein and calcium, these egg and salmon roll-ups are a firm family favourite. They can be stored in the fridge for up to 48 hours.

SERVES 4 CHILDREN

1 tbsp olive oil
4 free-range eggs
3 tsp finely chopped fresh chives
Black pepper, to taste
4 tbsp cream cheese
4 small slices smoked salmon

Place the olive oil in a medium-sized frying pan over a medium heat.

Whisk the eggs lightly with a fork in a small bowl then stir in the chives and some black pepper.

Pour half the egg mixture into the pan and cook it for 2–3 minutes to make a thin omelette, taking care when turning it to maintain its circle shape.

Lift it out with a fish slice and leave it to cool on a wooden board while you cook the remaining egg mixture.

Spread a quarter of the cream cheese over the surface of one omelette and then place 2 slices of smoked salmon on top. Spread a second layer of cream cheese over the salmon.

Roll it up and cut it into 4–6 pieces.

Repeat with the other omelette.

EGG-FREE

Use chickpea flour to make pancakes in place of the omelettes – blend 30g flour with 120ml of water and a pinch of salt. This makes enough batter for 2 roll-ups.

DAIRY-FREE

Use creamy oat fraîche, such as Oatly, instead of cream cheese.

FISH-FREE

Use turkey or chicken slices.

RICOTTA WITH POMEGRANATE SEEDS

CREAM CHEESE WITH BANANA, CINNAMON AND HONEY

MELTED CHEESE AND GRATED APPLE

PEANUT BUTTER WITH SLICED STRAWBERRIES

EGG, SMOKED SALMON AND DILL

SIX TOAST TOPPINGS

CHOPPED TOMATO WITH BASIL AND BALSAMIC VINEGAR

CHAPTER TWO

DELICIOUS DRINKS

RASPBERRY CHIA SMOOTHIE

GREEN MONSTER SMOOTHIE

SMOOTHIES

RASPBERRY CHIA SMOOTHIE

Raspberries are one of the healthiest fruits you can give your children. As well as being low in sugar, they are rich in fibre and flavonoids. Chia seeds are a fantastic source of calcium, fibre and omega 3 fatty acids – great for those who can't eat dairy or fish.

SERVES 2–3 CHILDREN

200g raspberries (fresh or frozen)
¼ pineapple, peeled and cored
1 tsp chia seeds
A few kale leaves, stalks removed
200ml whole milk

Combine all the ingredients in a food processor and blitz for about 45 seconds, or until the chia seeds have broken down and the mixture is nice and smooth.

Pour into glasses to serve.

GREEN MONSTER SMOOTHIE

Big and green but not scary! This sweet and tangy smoothie is full of essential nutrients. The pineapple provides a good dose of vitamin C, while ginger is known to have powerful antibacterial properties. The green ingredients – spinach and avocado – contain folate, which is critical for brain development and mood.

SERVES 2–3 CHILDREN

½ pineapple, peeled and cored
Handful of baby spinach leaves
½ avocado, peeled and stoned
Juice of ½ lime
Small knob of fresh root ginger, peeled
100–150ml water, if required

Add the pineapple, spinach, avocado, lime and ginger to a food processor and blitz for about 45 seconds, or until the mixture is nice and smooth.

Add some water if the smoothie needs thinning a little.

Pour into glasses to serve.

KEFIR TWO WAYS

Kefir is a wonder food! It is a key food for gut health, as well as immunity (see page 36). The great news is you can now find ready-made natural kefir in the milk aisle of many supermarkets. Blend it with the fruits below to make it more appealing for your children.

MANGO & PASSIONFRUIT

SERVES 1–2 CHILDREN
250ml kefir
1 mango, peeled and stoned
1 passionfruit, pulped

STRAWBERRY & HONEY

SERVES 1–2 CHILDREN
250ml kefir
200g strawberries, stalks removed
1 tsp runny honey

Measure the kefir and the flavourings of your choice into a blender and blitz until smooth. Pour into 1–2 glasses to serve.

DAIRY-FREE
Use coconut kefir which you can find online or at your local health food shop.

MANGO & PASSIONFRUIT
STRAWBERRY & HONEY

THREE FRUITY WATERS

Encouraging kids to drink enough fluids can be quite a challenge, so flavouring it by adding a smidgen of fruit, mint or even cucumber can help them drink their 6 glasses a day. You can pop the fruit into a water bottle at the start of the day and by the time they get to school the flavours will have infused. For parties, serve from a clear drinks dispenser with some slices of the fruit and it will beat sugary squash hands down.

ORANGE

SERVES 1 CHILD
Squeeze the juice of 1 orange into 500ml water.

RASPBERRY & MINT

SERVES 1 CHILD
Pop a few raspberries and the leaves from a sprig of mint into a 500ml bottle of water and leave to infuse for at least 30 minutes.

LIME & CUCUMBER

SERVES 1 CHILD
Squeeze the juice of half a lime into 500ml water and add a couple of slices of cucumber.

WATERMELON & MINT SLUSHY

This is a refreshing pink juice that you and your children will love. My nieces call it 'Princess Juice', and I agree that it is so amazingly good it really is fit for royalty.

SERVES 1–2 CHILDREN

3 thick slices watermelon, peeled and seeds removed
100ml coconut water
Handful of fresh mint leaves
4 ice cubes

Blitz all the ingredients together in a blender, pour into glasses and serve.

ZINGY CARROT JUICE

This is one of the first drinks I try with my fussiest patients. The zing from the ginger and lemon and the sweetness of the apples are a delicious combination. What's more, it's full of vitamin C, perfect for days when your kids are a bit sniffly or under the weather. You will need a vegetable juicer to make this one. (See photograph on page 92.)

ooooooo

SERVES 1–2 CHILDREN

Small knob of fresh root ginger, peeled
1 thick slice lemon, rind left on
2 apples
1 carrot

Push all the ingredients through the chute of your vegetable juicer, with the ginger and lemon sandwiched between the two apples.

Pour into glasses to serve.

BEDTIME TURMERIC MILK

Little kids love to have warm milk before bed and, as they get older, they like to have something a bit more grown up. This blend of turmeric and cinnamon warms and soothes the tummy and helps older kids and teens wind down after a busy day. You can increase the turmeric to ½ tsp once your child gets used to the taste. Like chocolate, turmeric has anti-inflammatory properties and adding a little bit of black pepper enhances its benefits. Promising studies are also showing that turmeric may be beneficial for chronic skin conditions and asthma.

SERVES 1–2 CHILDREN

235ml whole, almond or coconut milk
1 tsp runny honey
¼ tsp vanilla essence
¼ tsp ground cinnamon
¼ tsp ground turmeric
Few grinds of black pepper

Pour the milk into a small saucepan and stir in all the other ingredients.

Place the pan over a medium heat and warm it slowly until it is a suitable temperature for your child. To make it nice and frothy, whisk it for a few seconds before serving.

DAIRY-FREE

Use your child's favourite dairy-free milk, such as coconut or almond milk.

PROPER HOT CHOCOLATE

Hot chocolate should be an occasional treat rather than an everyday staple because of the sugar, but it can provide a lovely pep-up after a hard game of football or a long walk in the countryside. When you make hot chocolate from scratch, you can use ingredients you trust. Real chocolate is actually good for you. It contains polyphenols which have antioxidant and anti-inflammatory properties as well as magnesium; whereas some ready-made hot chocolate powders contain up to 23 different ingredients, including several E-numbers, artificial sweeteners and flavourings.

SERVES 1–2 CHILDREN

- 2 tsp raw cacao powder or cocoa powder
- 3 tsp coconut sugar or light muscovado sugar
- Mug of whole milk
- ½ tsp vanilla essence

Add the dry ingredients to a small saucepan and slowly mix in the milk and vanilla essence.

Place the pan over a medium heat and warm the mixture slowly until it is a suitable temperature for your child. If they want it nice and frothy, whisk it for a few seconds before serving.

DAIRY-FREE

Use your child's favourite dairy-free milk, such as hazelnut, cashew, almond or coconut.

CHAPTER THREE

HEARTY SOUPS

CREAMY HADDOCK & SWEETCORN CHOWDER

A meal-in-one with lots of veggies, this is a great after-school soup or a quick Saturday lunch that the whole family will love. (See photograph on previous page.)

SERVES A FAMILY OF 4–5

1 tbsp coconut oil (with a neutral flavour)
1 medium onion, chopped
1 garlic clove, diced
1 large potato, peeled and diced
1 carrot, peeled and diced
1 celery stick, trimmed and diced
100g red lentils
500ml fish stock
1 tsp medium curry powder
400ml coconut milk
2 undyed and naturally smoked haddock fillets
175g sweetcorn
Handful of baby spinach leaves, finely chopped

Place a saucepan over a medium heat, add the coconut oil and fry the onion until it is transparent. Add the garlic and fry for another minute.

Stir in the potato, carrot, celery and lentils, along with the fish stock, curry powder and coconut milk and bring it to the boil. Reduce the heat and leave it to simmer for around 20 minutes, or until the lentils are soft.

If your child prefers smooth soup, blitz it with a hand blender at this stage.

Add the haddock, sweetcorn and spinach and continue to simmer gently for a few minutes until the fish is cooked through. Season and gently break up the haddock with a fork.

You can prepare the soup base in advance and even freeze it. Once it has defrosted, reheat it and add the fish, sweetcorn and spinach.

CELERY-FREE

Use a leek instead.

FISH-FREE

Use chicken stock and 2 diced chicken breasts. Brown the chicken first then add it to the soup 10 minutes before the sweetcorn and spinach.

PEARLED FARRO COMFORT SOUP

This soup is full of bug-busting nutrients and vitamins and is our 'go-to' when anyone in the family gets a sniffle or a cough. Farro is a tasty Italian wholegrain alternative to rice. It is soft and juicy, and, like risotto rice, absorbs stock and flavours beautifully. It is also nutritious and easy to digest. I have used chicken thighs rather than breast here because they are richer in iron, and also a bit cheaper.

SERVES A FAMILY OF 4–5

- 1 tbsp olive oil or butter
- 6 chicken thighs, boneless and skinless, cut into small pieces
- 3 rashers of smoked bacon or 100g pancetta, finely chopped
- 1 leek, trimmed and finely chopped
- 3 garlic cloves, crushed
- 1 bay leaf
- 2 tsp mixed Mediterranean herbs
- 100g pearled farro*
- 500ml fresh chicken stock or bone broth (see page 59)
- 1 carrot, peeled and finely chopped
- 1 tbsp finely chopped parsley

* You can use pearled spelt as an alternative to farro. It takes much longer to cook but is just as delicious and nutritious.

Place a large saucepan over a medium heat, add the olive oil and brown the chicken and bacon for 8–10 minutes, turning occasionally.

Tip in the leek and garlic, followed by the herbs and cook for another minute. Finally, stir in the farro and the chicken stock.

Bring it up to the boil, reduce the heat and simmer for 12–15 minutes, stirring from time to time.

Add the carrot a couple of minutes before the end of the cooking time so it remains crunchy.

Scatter the soup with parsley and season to taste with salt and black pepper before serving.

GLUTEN-FREE

Use brown risotto rice or buckwheat groats – cooking times will vary so read the instructions on the packet.

RED LENTIL, PEPPER & TOMATO SOUP

The 'hidden' lentils blended into this soup make it a much heartier meal than plain tomato soup. Roasting tomatoes and peppers gives a deep sweet flavour that kids love. And did you know that cooked tomatoes provide more of the antioxidant lycopene than raw tomatoes? Lycopene, when combined with vitamin A (found in abundance in carrots), can help improve asthma symptoms.

SERVES A FAMILY OF 4–5

1 tbsp olive oil
800g (6–8 large) plum or beef tomatoes
1 onion, quartered
2 garlic cloves
1 carrot, peeled and quartered lengthwise
1 red pepper, deseeded and roughly chopped
100g red lentils
200ml fresh chicken or vegetable stock
Handful of fresh basil leaves, torn
Optional extras: grated Parmesan, green pesto* and olive oil

* See page 124 to learn how to make super-speedy *Sunflower Pesto*.

Preheat the oven to 180°C/160°C fan/gas mark 4.

Add the olive oil to a roasting tin and place it in the oven to heat up.

Plunge the tomatoes into boiling water for a couple of minutes to split the skins and make them easy to peel.

Peel the tomatoes and cut them in half. Place them cut side down in the hot roasting tin with the onion, garlic cloves, carrot and red pepper. Cover the tin with parchment paper and return to the oven for 25–35 minutes.

Meanwhile, measure the lentils into a large saucepan and pour in the chicken stock. Place the pan over a medium heat and cook until the lentils are soft, about 15–18 minutes.

Remove the vegetables from the oven and squeeze the flesh out of the garlic cloves, discarding the skin.

Tip the vegetables into the pan with the lentils, add the fresh basil and blitz everything together with a blender.

Season to taste and add Parmesan, pesto or olive oil, if using.

CHICKEN NOODLE MISO SOUP

This soup suits older kids and those who love spicy, flavoursome foods. It's one of the most popular recipes for my gang at home and is super quick to make.

SERVES A FAMILY OF 4–5

- 1 tbsp sesame oil
- 6 chicken thighs, boneless and skinless, cut into bite-size pieces
- 6 spring onions, trimmed and finely sliced
- 1 red pepper, deseeded and finely diced
- 150g broccoli, cut into florets
- 5cm knob of fresh root ginger, peeled and finely chopped
- 2 tbsp tamari soy sauce
- 2 tbsp light miso paste or 2 packets miso soup mix
- ½ red chilli, deseeded and finely diced
- 500ml fresh chicken stock or bone broth (see page 59)
- 250g brown rice noodles or vermicelli
- 1 carrot, peeled and cut into wide strips with a potato peeler
- 2 tbsp fresh coriander leaves
- Juice of ½ lime

Place a large saucepan over a high heat. Add the sesame oil and chicken and brown for 8–10 minutes, turning occasionally.

Add the spring onions, red pepper, broccoli, ginger, tamari, miso and red chilli and stir in the chicken stock. Bring to the boil.

Add the noodles and cook them according to the instructions on the packet, putting in the carrot a couple of minutes before the end.

Serve the soup with a scattering of coriander leaves and a squeeze of lime.

SOYA-FREE

Use coconut aminos instead of tamari soy sauce, and use soya-free miso, which is made from rice and koji culture, both available from health food shops.

SESAME-FREE

Use olive or coconut oil instead.

WATERMELON GAZPACHO

A refreshing no-cook soup for a hot summer's day. It can be made in just a few minutes and is gorgeous served with crusty wholemeal bread.

SERVES A FAMILY OF 4–5

- 4 large ripe plum tomatoes
- 3 spring onions, trimmed and roughly chopped
- 1 garlic clove, roughly chopped
- ⅓ small cucumber, peeled
- 300g watermelon, peeled, deseeded and cut into chunks
- 1 red pepper, deseeded
- 1 tbsp red wine vinegar
- 1 tbsp fresh parsley leaves, plus extra to garnish
- 150ml extra-virgin olive oil, plus extra for drizzling or olive oil hearts

Plunge the tomatoes into boiling water for a couple of minutes to split the skins and make them easy to peel.

Peel the tomatoes and add to a food processor with all the ingredients, except the olive oil. Blitz until smooth.

Season to taste with salt and black pepper, then keep the blender running as you slowly pour in the olive oil.

The gazpacho can be stored in the fridge for up to 48 hours. Serve it cold with a drizzle of olive oil or a frozen olive oil heart* and a scattering of fresh parsley.

*To make olive oil hearts, freeze some extra-virgin olive oil in a heart-shaped silicone ice cube tray. Then pop them out of the tray and store them in a small container in the freezer. You could also make olive oil stars and other shapes.

CHAPTER FOUR

SIMPLE SUPPERS

MINI TOAD IN THE HOLE

Light and fluffy but without the white flour, this toad in the hole is sure to be a hit with the family. Omit the sausages and you have amazing Yorkshire puddings, perfect for your Sunday roast.

SERVES A FAMILY OF 4–5

Olive oil for greasing the tin
24 mini sausages (or 12 chipolatas twisted in the middle and cut in two)
100g chickpea flour*
2 free-range eggs
240ml whole milk
1 heaped tbsp finely chopped rosemary
½ tsp fine sea salt

* Chickpea flour, also known as besan or gram flour, can be found in the Asian section of large supermarkets and Asian shops and is a good-value source of protein.

Preheat the oven to 180°C/160°C fan/gas mark 4 and grease a roasting tin with a little olive oil.

Place the sausages in the tin and cook for 15 minutes – remove from the oven half-cooked.

Increase the oven temperature to 220°C/200°C fan/gas mark 7 and generously grease a 12-hole muffin tin.

Meanwhile, mix the chickpea flour with the eggs in a large measuring jug, then slowly stir in the milk a little at a time to prevent any lumps forming.

Add the chopped rosemary and the salt.

Place the muffin tin in the oven to heat up.

When it is sizzling hot, half fill each hole with batter and then pop two mini sausages inside.

Return the tin to the oven to cook for 18–20 minutes, or until the batter has risen and is golden and fluffy.

Serve the mini toad in the holes with lots of green vegetables.

GLUTEN-FREE
Use gluten-free sausages.

DAIRY-FREE
Use oat milk.

FIVE VEG SHEPHERD'S PIE

A traditional British pie that's a winner with kids. We all love mashed potato but on its own it can cause our blood sugars to shoot up. This is why we like it combined with swede and lots of butter and milk to slow the release of energy. More veg equals more gut-friendly fibre, too. You can make the mash from a mix of other root vegetables – sweet potato, celeriac or carrots work well – make sure to include at least one potato in the blend for the right consistency.

SERVES A FAMILY OF 4–5

- 6–8 medium potatoes, peeled and quartered
- 1 small swede, peeled and diced
- 1–2 tbsp butter
- 50–100ml whole milk
- 1 tbsp olive oil
- 1 onion, finely chopped
- 400–500g lamb mince
- 2–3 carrots, peeled and diced
- 1 leek, trimmed and finely chopped
- 3–4 tsp finely chopped fresh rosemary
- 1–2 tbsp Worcestershire sauce

Place the potatoes and swede in a large saucepan of boiling water and boil for 10–15 minutes, until they are soft. Drain them, then mash them and stir in the butter and milk.

Meanwhile, place another large saucepan over a gentle heat, add the olive oil and fry the onion for 3–4 minutes, or until it is soft.

Tip in the lamb, turn up the heat and brown it for 8–10 minutes.

Reduce the temperature and add the carrots, leek, rosemary and Worcestershire sauce.

Preheat the grill to its highest setting.

When the carrots are soft, season the mixture with salt and black pepper, then pour it into a family-size heatproof dish. Spread the mash evenly over the top with a fork and place under the hot grill to crisp up the topping.

GLUTEN-FREE

Opt for a gluten-free Worcestershire sauce, such as Biona.

DAIRY-FREE

Use dairy-free spread and oat milk.

VEG-LOADED BEEF BOLOGNAISE

If my kids have been away from home for a few days, this is the meal they miss the most and always ask for on their return. It contains 6 different veg which can all be grated or finely chopped for fussy eaters. You can also add lentils and/or organic chicken livers to boost the iron content.

SERVES A FAMILY OF 4–5

- 1 tbsp olive oil
- 1 onion, finely chopped
- 500g beef mince
- 4 rashers of streaky bacon, finely chopped, or 100g bacon lardons
- 2 garlic cloves, crushed
- 1 carrot, peeled and diced
- 1 celery stick, trimmed and diced
- ½ courgette, very finely chopped
- ½ red pepper, deseeded and very finely chopped
- 2 x 400g tins chopped tomatoes
- 1 bay leaf
- 1 heaped tbsp mixed Mediterranean herbs

Place a large saucepan over a gentle heat, add the olive oil and fry the onion until it is soft.

Add the mince and bacon, increase the heat and brown the meat.

Turn down the heat to medium and stir in the garlic. Cook for 1 minute, then add the remaining ingredients. Let the sauce simmer gently for at least 45 minutes (the longer the better), giving it a stir from time to time.

Check the seasoning and serve it with freshly cooked wholemeal pasta.

CELERY-FREE

Use fennel instead.

TURMERIC KEDGEREE

My mum's kedgeree is a legend in our house. Traditionally, kedgeree was served at breakfast, but you can eat it at any time of the day. This recipe brings together the gorgeous combination of buttery, delicately curried rice, smoky haddock and hardboiled eggs. I have added some peas for sweetness, but otherwise it's the same kedgeree that she used to cook for us as children.

SERVES A FAMILY OF 4–5

250g brown basmati rice
100g peas
3 free-range eggs
1 tbsp butter or ghee
125ml whole milk
¼ tsp ground turmeric
1 heaped tsp mild or medium curry powder
200g undyed and naturally smoked haddock or salmon
1 tbsp roughly chopped fresh parsley
Cayenne pepper (optional)

Cook the rice as per the packet instructions. In the last 2 minutes of cooking, add the peas.

Meanwhile, bring a small saucepan of water to the boil and carefully place the eggs in. Boil them for 10 minutes, then remove from the heat and run them under a cold tap to cool them, before peeling and cutting them into quarters.

Melt the butter in a large frying pan over a medium heat.

Add the milk, turmeric and curry powder and bring it up to a simmer.

Add the fish to the milky mixture, cover with a lid and cook gently for 5 minutes. Turn off the heat and leave the fish to continue cooking in the hot milk.

Break the fish up gently with a fork then place in a serving dish with the rice. Add some of the milk from the pan if you like it creamy. Season with plenty of salt and black pepper.

Place the eggs on top of the kedgeree and scatter over some chopped parsley. You can add a sprinkle of cayenne pepper for extra spice.

EGG-FREE

Use some finely chopped baby spinach leaves and a handful of North Atlantic prawns instead.

DAIRY-FREE

Use dairy-free spread and oat milk.

SUNFLOWER PESTO

This is a nut-free pesto that is delicious with pasta. It also makes a great dip for veg sticks – handy for packed lunches. Nuts such as walnuts, almonds and pine kernels work beautifully here, too, so swap around as much as you like.

MAKES 4–5 SERVINGS

30g fresh basil
50g Parmesan, grated
1 garlic clove, crushed
30g sunflower seeds
60ml light olive oil

Blitz all the ingredients together in a food processor for 2 minutes.

DAIRY-FREE

Use a vegan Parmesan alternative, such as Violife Prosociano or add a pinch of salt and some more sunflower seeds and garlic instead.

La Española
SPANISH
OLIVE OIL
Desde
1840

CHICKEN PASTA PESTO
WITH FRESH TOMATOES

When my kids were little, I could hide almost any new food in pesto and they would eat it. They still adore fresh pesto and one of their favourite dishes is this chicken pasta with lots of fresh chopped tomatoes. It's quick to make, and if there are any leftovers it makes a delicious alternative to sandwiches for a packed lunch.

SERVES A FAMILY OF 4–5

200g wholemeal pasta
1 tbsp olive oil
2 chicken breasts, skinless, cut into small chunks
4 tbsp *Sunflower Pesto* (see page 124)
Handful of baby spinach leaves, finely chopped
200g mini cherry or plum tomatoes, halved or quartered
1 tbsp extra-virgin olive oil

Cook the pasta according to the packet instructions.

Meanwhile, place a large frying pan over a medium heat, add the oil and fry the chicken gently for 10–12 minutes, or until it is slightly browned and cooked through.

Tip the chicken into a large bowl and mix in the pesto and spinach, followed by the cooked pasta and tomatoes.

Drizzle over the extra-virgin olive oil to finish.

CRUNCHY LEMON CHICKEN GOUJONS

Faster to cook than a frozen chicken nugget and much more nutritious. These are a hit with picky eaters drawn to crunchy beige food.

SERVES A FAMILY OF 4–5

- 4–5 large chicken breasts, skinless
- 120g chickpea flour or wholemeal flour
- 2 free-range eggs, beaten
- 120g ground almonds
- 60g Parmesan or Pecorino, finely grated
- Zest of 2 lemons
- 1–2 tbsp olive oil or large knob of coconut oil (with a neutral flavour)

Cut each chicken breast through the middle into two thin slices, then cut these slices vertically into goujons.

Pat them dry with a piece of kitchen paper.

Prepare three plates – the first with the flour, the second with the beaten egg and the third with a mixture of almonds, Parmesan and lemon zest.

Dip each goujon in the flour, then the egg and finally the cheesy lemony mix. Place them on a clean plate until ready to cook.

Place a frying pan over a medium heat, add the oil and leave until it is sizzling.

Using tongs, carefully place each goujon in the pan and brown them, turning them every few minutes. Depending on the thickness of the chicken, they should take around 8–12 minutes to cook through.

Remove from the pan with the tongs and serve with *Omega Mayo* (see page 131), *Smart Sweet Potato Chips* (see page 130) and a salad or peas.

GLUTEN-FREE
Use gluten-free or chickpea flour (also known as besan or gram).

NUT-FREE
Use ground red lentils instead of the ground almonds. Simply grind them up (raw) in a coffee grinder.

EGG-FREE
Dip the chicken in milk instead of egg.

DAIRY-FREE
Use a vegan Parmesan alternative, such as Violife Prosociano.

SMART SWEET POTATO CHIPS

All children love chips! The problem is that most chips are deep-fried in pro-inflammatory vegetable oils. Sweet potatoes are a great alternative to white potatoes as they release their energy more slowly. Cooking them in coconut oil also provides a good dose of healthy brain fuel. I've added rosemary because it has so many health-boosting properties, improving memory and sleep, and also helping the body absorb vitamin D, which is essential to mood, immunity and well-being.

SERVES A FAMILY OF 4–5

- 4 sweet potatoes, peeled and sliced into thin chips
- 2 tbsp coconut oil (with a neutral flavour), melted
- 4 tsp finely chopped fresh rosemary leaves or 2 tsp dried rosemary
- 1 tsp fine sea salt

Preheat the oven to 200°C/180°C fan/gas mark 5/6.

Soak the chips in water for 20 minutes to draw out the excess starch. This will help make them crispy on the outside and soft on the inside.

Pat the chips dry with a kitchen towel, then tip them into a bowl and toss them in the melted coconut oil.

Sprinkle the rosemary and salt over the chips and place them on a baking tray, ensuring there is plenty of space in between each one.

Bake them in the oven for 35 minutes, turning them from time to time.

OMEGA MAYO

Omega 3 is a key brain food and the best source is oily fish. The problem is that many kids do not eat fish, or certainly not enough of it. This omega 3-rich mayonnaise is a good way of increasing it in your child's diet. All the family will love dipping their chicken goujons and sweet potato chips in it. It goes equally well with prawns, steak, veg sticks or boiled eggs. I try to always have some in the fridge instead of regular mayo.

MAKES ABOUT 200ML

- 2 free-range egg yolks (at room temperature)
- 1 garlic clove, finely chopped
- ½ tsp anchovy paste or 1 anchovy
- Juice of ½–1 lemon
- Pinch of salt and black pepper
- 40ml avocado oil (at room temperature)
- 40ml flaxseed oil (at room temperature)
- 80ml cold-pressed rapeseed oil (at room temperature)

Using an electric whisk or hand blender, whisk the egg yolks, garlic, anchovy, lemon juice and salt and pepper together in a bowl.

Mix the three oils together in a jug and pour them into the egg mixture drip by drip, whisking all the time, until it becomes thick and creamy.

FISH-FREE

Replace the anchovy with 1 tsp Dijon mustard.

FISHY FRIDAYS

Fish fingers with a healthy twist. The coating is made with ground red lentils, which go bright orange when they are cooked with turmeric and paprika. Crunchy and delicious with not a hint of white flour or breadcrumbs, these are an excellent way of getting some extra fibre and iron into an ultra-picky eater. Serve them with *Cheesy Courgette Chips* (see page 134).

SERVES A FAMILY OF 4–5

- 4 cod steaks, cut into 2cm strips
- 100g red lentils
- ¼ tsp paprika
- ¼ tsp ground turmeric
- 60g chickpea or wholemeal flour
- 1 free-range egg, beaten
- 1 tbsp olive oil or a knob of coconut oil (with a neutral flavour)

Pat the cod strips dry with kitchen paper.

Measure the lentils, paprika and turmeric into a food processor, season with salt and pepper, and blitz with the grinding blade until you have a fine flour.

Set out three plates – the first for the flour, the second for the egg and the third for the red lentil mixture. Dip the cod strips into the flour, then the egg and finally into the red lentil mixture.

Place a large frying pan over a medium heat, add the oil and leave until it is sizzling.

Using tongs, carefully place the cod strips in the pan and cook them for a few minutes on all sides, or until the fish is cooked all the way through and the batter is crispy and slightly browned.

CHEESY COURGETTE CHIPS

Try these delicious courgette chips as an alternative to boring potato chips. Perfect with a dollop of *My Super-Healthy Ketchup* (see page opposite).

SERVES A FAMILY OF 4–5

- 1 large courgette, cut into long, thin strips
- 50g spelt or wholemeal flour
- 1 free-range egg, beaten
- 50g fine oatmeal
- 50g Cheddar, grated
- 2 tsp mixed Mediterranean herbs
- 1 tbsp olive oil

Preheat the oven to 180°C/160°C fan/gas mark 4.

Pat the courgette dry with kitchen paper.

Set out three plates: the first for the flour and the second for the egg. For the third plate, mix together the oatmeal, Cheddar and herbs and season with salt and black pepper.

Dip each courgette strip into the flour, then the egg and finally into the oatmeal mixture.

Lay the strips on a greased baking tray and bake them in the oven for 25 minutes, or until they are golden brown.

GLUTEN-FREE

Use gluten-free plain flour or chickpea flour, and gluten-free oats.

EGG-FREE

Dip the courgette strips in buttermilk or milk instead of egg.

DAIRY-FREE

Use a vegan Parmesan alternative, such as Violife Prosociano.

MY SUPER-HEALTHY KETCHUP

Ketchup is one of the nation's favourite condiments. Vast quantities of it are consumed every year. It is a big source of hidden sugar in children's diets but you can easily make a healthy version yourself with four simple ingredients.

MAKES ABOUT 350ML

500g passata
20ml apple cider vinegar
60ml runny honey
¼ tsp mixed spice

Measure all the ingredients into a saucepan with tall sides (to stop the sauce from spitting everywhere) and place over a medium heat.

Bring to the boil, reduce the temperature and leave to simmer for 12 minutes, or until the mixture has reduced by about half and is nice and thick.

You can then add more water and let it bubble away for longer if you want to give it a deeper taste.

Leave to cool and store in a jar in the refrigerator.

CHINESE GINGER CHICKEN
WITH BROWN NOODLES

A quick and tasty lunch or supper that is perfect for overtired kids and parents. It's stuffed with immune-supporting ingredients, such as ginger and garlic, and vitamin C-rich lemon juice and peppers. You can buy wholegrain brown rice noodles in most supermarkets now but buckwheat noodles or even brown rice work just as well. Try replacing the chicken with prawns or pork, too.

SERVES A FAMILY OF 4–5

- 2 tbsp sesame oil
- 1 small onion, finely chopped
- 1 garlic clove, crushed
- 2 chicken breasts, skinless, diced
- 1 carrot, peeled and finely chopped
- 1 courgette, finely chopped
- 1 red pepper, deseeded and finely chopped
- 1 heaped tsp finely chopped fresh root ginger
- 225g (1 packet) brown rice noodles
- 1 tbsp tamari soy sauce
- 1 tbsp fresh lemon juice

Place a large frying pan over a low heat, add the sesame oil and fry the onion for 2–3 minutes, or until it is soft.

Add the garlic and cook for 1 minute before stirring in the chicken. Cook it for 2–3 minutes, then stir in the rest of the vegetables and the ginger.

Continue to cook over a medium heat for 10 minutes, or until the vegetables have softened.

Meanwhile, cook the noodles according to the packet instructions.

Add the tamari and lemon juice to the vegetables, then stir in the drained noodles and combine all the ingredients well.

SOYA-FREE
Use coconut aminos or coconut teriyaki sauce instead of tamari soy sauce.

SESAME-FREE
Use coconut oil (with a neutral flavour).

HADDOCK & SALMON FISH PIE

A warming, nourishing dish that reminds me of my childhood. It is filled with omega 3-rich goodies and lots of hidden veg.

MAKES ENOUGH FOR 3–4 LITTLE PIES

- 2–3 medium potatoes, peeled and cut into chunks
- 30g unsalted butter
- 1 leek, trimmed and very finely chopped
- 1 tsp plain wholemeal flour
- 200ml whole milk
- 1 undyed and naturally smoked haddock fillet, cut into 2cm cubes
- 1 salmon fillet, cut into 2cm cubes
- 1 medium courgette, grated
- 1 free-range egg, hardboiled and chopped

Preheat the oven to 180°C/160°C fan/gas mark 4.

Bring a large saucepan of salted water to the boil and cook the potatoes for 10–15 minutes, or until they are soft. Drain then mash them with half the butter. Put them to one side.

Melt half the remaining butter in another saucepan over a low heat. Add the leek and fry it gently for 4 minutes.

Stir the flour into the leek, then slowly add the milk, stirring well to prevent lumps forming.

Tip in all the cubed fish and poach it for around 5 minutes, or until it is cooked.

Strain off any excess liquid then stir in the grated courgette, chopped egg and season with black pepper.

Divide the mixture between 3–4 little pie dishes then spread the mashed potato over the top. Bake them in the oven for about 20 minutes, or until the potato is golden brown.

GLUTEN-FREE

Use gluten-free plain flour.

EGG-FREE

Add a few prawns and finely chopped spinach instead of the egg.

DAIRY-FREE

Use dairy-free spread and oat milk.

CHAPTER FIVE

MIGHTY MAINS

CHICKEN & SPINACH CURRY

Most kids love tasty food and sometimes what we offer them is too simple or bland. Cooked spinach, for instance, tends not to be very popular with kids if it is served plain on the side of a plate. However, if it is finely chopped and mixed with delicious Indian curry spices, it becomes a winner dinner.

SERVES A FAMILY OF 4–5

1 tbsp coconut oil (with a neutral flavour)
1 onion, finely chopped
2 garlic cloves, crushed
2 heaped tsp fresh root ginger, finely chopped
2 tsp ground cumin
2 tsp ground turmeric
6 cardamom pods, seeds only
Pinch of black pepper
4 chicken breasts, skinless, diced
400ml coconut milk
2 tsp coconut sugar or light muscovado sugar
4 blocks frozen spinach or 2 handfuls of spinach leaves, finely chopped

Place a large frying pan over a low heat, add the coconut oil and fry the onion for 5 minutes, or until it is soft.

Stir in the garlic, ginger and spices.

Add the chicken and cook it gently for 12 minutes, or until cooked through.

Pour in the coconut milk and stir in the sugar. Continue to cook for 3–4 minutes before adding the spinach. This should take just a few minutes to defrost and cook in the sauce. Season to taste.

Serve with brown rice and mini poppadoms.

MEAT-FREE

Replace the chicken with a 400g tin of chickpeas, drained and rinsed.

PULLED DUCK
WITH PERSIAN COLESLAW & CAULI COUSCOUS

Duck is probably my family's favourite meat. It is tasty and tender, especially when it has been slow-cooked and pulled. It can be on the pricey side, so we snap up a couple when they are half-price in the supermarket and pop them in the freezer. You can make amazing stock from the bones to turn into soups. Baharat is a popular Persian spice mix containing a delicious combination of paprika, coriander, black pepper, cumin, cinnamon, cayenne, cloves, nutmeg and cardamom – lots of clever spices for keeping tummies happy.

SERVES A FAMILY OF 4–5

1 whole duck *
1 tbsp Baharat Persian spice mix (such as Bart's)

For the dressing:
2 tbsp olive oil
Juice of 1 lime
Handful of fresh mint leaves, finely chopped
Handful of fresh coriander leaves, finally chopped
1 red chilli, deseeded and sliced (optional)
Pinch of fine sea salt

2 little-gem lettuces, washed

* If you want to speed things up, use duck legs, which take only 2 hours to cook.

Preheat the oven to 150°C/130°C fan/gas mark 2.

Rub the spice mix into the duck and place it on a roasting rack over an oven tray. This will collect the fat as it cooks. Roast it in the oven for 3–4 hours, depending on the size, turning it every hour.

Meanwhile, combine the dressing ingredients in a small bowl and lightly whisk together.

Remove the duck from the oven once it is cooked through and let it stand for a few minutes. Then pull the flesh off the bones using two forks and place in a large bowl.

Toss it in the tangy dressing and serve it in a lettuce leaf with *Persian Coleslaw* and *Cauli Couscous with Pomegranate Seeds* on the side (see page 146).

PERSIAN COLESLAW

A creamy side for burgers, chicken nuggets or fish fingers, as well as pulled duck. A great way to get three servings of fruit and veg in one hit.

SERVES A FAMILY OF 4–5

½ small pointed cabbage, shredded
4 medium carrots, peeled and grated
2 apples, cored and grated 3 heaped tbsp plain Greek yoghurt
3 heaped tbsp mayonnaise
1 heaped tbsp ground sumac
1 heaped tbsp cumin seeds (or ground cumin)

Place the cabbage, carrots and apples in a large bowl.

Pour the yoghurt, mayonnaise, sumac and cumin seeds over the vegetables and mix everything together well.

CAULI COUSCOUS
WITH POMEGRANATE SEEDS

A simple way of getting more veg and fibre into your kids. The gem-like pomegranate seeds are bursting with health-boosting polyphenols.

SERVES A FAMILY OF 4–5

1 whole cauliflower,
1 tbsp coconut oil (with a neutral flavour)
2 tbsp water
1 pomegranate or 125g fresh pomegranate seeds
Handful of fresh parsley, leaves finely chopped
Handful of unsalted pistachios, shelled

Core the cauliflower and discard the outer leaves. Place it in a food processor and blitz into couscous-sized pieces.

Place the coconut oil and water in a large saucepan over a medium heat. Add the cauliflower and cook it for 4–5 minutes with the lid on, stirring every minute or so.

Transfer the cauliflower to a large serving bowl and allow it to cool slightly. Season and sprinkle over the pomegranate seeds, parsley, pistachios.

FRUITY FETA SALAD

This is a perfect balance of salty and sweet that is cool and refreshing on a hot summer's day. Another lunchbox or picnic winner as there is no dressing.

SERVES 4–5

- 200g feta, diced
- 6 cherry or baby plum tomatoes, halved or quartered
- 1 thick slice of watermelon, peeled, deseeded and diced (optional)
- ½ cucumber, diced
- 2 tbsp pitted olives
- 1 tbsp fresh mint, finely chopped

Simply combine all the ingredients together in a salad bowl, toss gently and serve.

DAIRY-FREE
Use diced tofu marinated in lemon juice and salt, or cubes of vegan cheese.

TZATZIKI

A zesty yoghurt dip that is useful to have at the ready for hungry fridge-raiders as it is wonderful with chopped raw veg. It's delicious with falafels and wholemeal pittas, but try it with lamb meatballs, beef burgers or chicken patties too.

SERVES 4–5

- 4 heaped tbsp plain Greek yoghurt
- 1 tbsp peeled and finely chopped cucumber
- 2 heaped tsp finely chopped fresh mint leaves
- 1 garlic clove, crushed
- Squeeze of lemon
- Pinch of fine sea salt and black pepper

Simply combine all the ingredients together in a bowl.

DAIRY-FREE
Use oat crème fraîche, such as Oatly, instead of yoghurt.

FALAFELS THREE WAYS

These falafels are a great source of vegetarian protein and fibre. There are three delicious flavours – Apple, Sun-Dried Tomato and Olive – and they make perfect nibbles for lunchboxes or a more substantial feast if served with wholemeal pitta bread. They are free of allergens (apart from sesame seeds) so a good option to serve at birthday parties.

MAKES 18 FALAFELS (6 OF EACH FLAVOUR)

2 x 400g tins chickpeas, drained and rinsed
4 tbsp chickpea flour
2 tsp baking powder
1 onion, very finely chopped
2 garlic cloves, finely chopped
1 large sprig of parsley, leaves finely chopped
2 tsp ground cumin
2 tsp ground coriander
20ml light olive oil, plus extra for greasing
Pinch of fine sea salt
4 sun-dried tomatoes, puréed in a blender
10 Kalamata olives, stoned and puréed in a blender
½ small apple, grated
4 tbsp sesame seeds (optional)

Preheat the oven to 180°C/160°C fan/gas mark 4 and line a baking tray with parchment paper.

Blitz the chickpeas, chickpea flour, baking powder, onion, garlic, parsley, cumin, coriander, olive oil and salt in a food processor until you have a thick paste.

Divide the mixture between three bowls and fold the sun-dried tomato paste into one bowl and the olive paste into another. Squeeze the juice out of the grated apple with your hands before adding the pulp to the third bowl.

Shape each mixture into balls then roll them in the sesame seeds, if using, and place them on the baking tray. Flatten them slightly to increase their surface area so they crisp up better then brush each one with a little olive oil.

Put the tray in the fridge for at least 15 minutes to firm up the falafels, then bake them in the oven for 20–30 minutes, turning them carefully halfway through.

Serve them with *Tzatziki, Fruity Feta Salad* (see page 147) and warm wholemeal pitta bread.

The falafels can be stored in the fridge for up to 3 days.

OLIVE
APPLE
SUN-DRIED TOMATO

CHICKEN & THYME MEATBALLS
WITH A RED PEPPER SAUCE & SPAGHETTI

These are a great healthy alternative to the ones you buy in shops, which are generally over-processed. The red pepper sauce is smoky with a slight kick.

SERVES A FAMILY OF 4–5

For the meatballs:
2 tbsp olive oil or coconut oil (with a neutral flavour)
1 onion, finely chopped
½ courgette, finely grated
2 garlic cloves, diced
2 tsp finely chopped fresh thyme leaves
2 chicken breasts, skinless, diced
1 free-range egg

For the sauce:
1 tbsp olive oil or coconut oil (with a neutral flavour)
1 onion, finely chopped
1 red pepper, deseeded and finely chopped
3 garlic cloves, diced
1 tsp paprika
400g passata

200g wholemeal spaghetti
1 tbsp Parmesan, grated (optional)

For the meatballs, place a large frying pan over a medium heat, add 1 tbsp oil and fry the onion, courgette, garlic and thyme for around 5 minutes.

Remove from the heat and allow to cool before placing this mixture in a food processor with the diced chicken and egg and season. Blend it for about 1 minute, or until the chicken is minced and you can easily shape the mixture into little walnut-sized balls. It should make about 24 meatballs.

Leave the meatballs in the fridge for about 30 minutes to bind.

Meanwhile, make the red pepper sauce. Place a saucepan over a medium heat, add the oil and fry the onion, red pepper, garlic and some paprika for 3–4 minutes to soften them. Add the passata and simmer for 30–40 minutes until well-reduced.

Cook the spaghetti according to the packet instructions.

Meanwhile, place a large frying pan over a medium heat, add 1 tbsp oil and fry the meatballs for around 10 minutes, or until they are nicely browned and cooked through.

Drain the spaghetti and place on a large serving dish. Pile the meatballs on top, dollop with the red pepper sauce and scatter with grated Parmesan, if using.

GLUTEN-FREE

Use gluten-free spaghetti or pasta made from lentils or chickpeas.

EGG-FREE

Use 1 tbsp ground flaxseeds mixed with 2½ tbsp water to help bind the meatballs.

BLACK BEAN CHILLI

Perfect for meat-free Mondays. Black beans are one of nature's best sources of iron. Combined with wholegrain brown rice, they contain the same complete protein profile as meat.

SERVES 2–3 CHILDREN

1 tbsp olive oil
1 small onion, finely sliced
1 carrot, peeled and finely diced
3 tbsp tomato concentrate
100ml water
2 tsp paprika
2 tsp ground cumin
2 tsp ground coriander
1 bay leaf
2 x 400g tins black beans, drained

Place a large saucepan over a medium heat, add the olive oil and fry the onion gently for 3–4 minutes.

Add the carrot and, after a minute, stir in the tomato concentrate and water. Cook for a couple more minutes, then add the herbs, spices and black beans.

Bring the chilli to the boil then reduce the heat and leave it to simmer with the lid loosely on for 20 minutes, adding a little extra water if it gets dry.

Serve it with corn tortilla chips or brown rice and my fruity salsa or a dollop of yoghurt on the side.

MANGO & STRAWBERRY SALSA

My salsa is an exotic alternative to the traditional tomato-based version.

OOOOOOO

SERVES 2–3 CHILDREN

1 mango, peeled and diced
100g strawberries, sliced
2 spring onions, trimmed and finely sliced
Small handful of fresh coriander, finely chopped
Juice of ½ lime

Simply combine all the ingredients together in a bowl and mix well.

Try adding some finely chopped green chilli for some extra zing.

CHICKEN, CHORIZO & FLAGEOLET BEAN STEW

This rich aromatic stew makes a perfect warm supper on a winter's evening, and tastes even better the next day. Look out for nitrate/nitrite-free chorizo in your supermarket as this adds a lovely deep, smoky flavour to this tasty stew.

SERVES 2–3 CHILDREN

- 1 tbsp olive oil
- 2 chicken breasts, cut into bite-sized pieces
- 1 small onion, finely chopped
- 1 garlic clove, crushed
- 100g chorizo, finely chopped
- 1 red pepper, deseeded and roughly chopped
- 1 tsp smoked paprika
- 1 tsp fennel seeds
- 1 tsp ground cumin
- 2 tsp dried rosemary or 1 tbsp finely chopped fresh rosemary leaves
- 1 celery stick, trimmed and diced
- 1 medium carrot, peeled and diced
- 2 x 400g tins chopped tomatoes
- 1 x 400g tin flageolet or cannellini beans
- 2 tbsp fresh parsley leaves, roughly chopped

Place a large saucepan over a medium heat, add the olive oil and brown the chicken, then set aside.

Fry the onion in the remaining oil for 3–4 minutes.

Add the garlic and fry for another minute before stirring in the chorizo, red pepper, paprika, fennel seeds, cumin and rosemary. Stir well for a minute or so, then add the celery and carrot.

Stir in the browned chicken, followed by the tomatoes and beans. Bring to the boil, reduce the heat and leave it to simmer half covered for 45 minutes.

Scatter with parsley before serving.

It goes well with Rosemary & Garlic Hassleback Potatoes (see opposite) or brown rice and freshly steamed vegetables.

ROSEMARY & GARLIC HASSELBACK POTATOES

Kids love making hasselback potatoes and they go really well with all kinds of stews and roast meats.

SERVES 2–3 CHILDREN

1 tbsp olive oil
Large knob of butter
2–3 potatoes, one per person
Pinch of fine sea salt
1–2 garlic cloves, finely chopped
1 small sprig of rosemary per potato, leaves finely chopped

Preheat the oven to 180°C/160°C fan/gas mark 4.

Put the olive oil and butter in a roasting tin and place it in the oven to heat up.

Place two wooden spoons on a chopping board and put a potato between the handles. Cut a series of vertical slits downwards into the potato, 2mm apart. The spoon handles will prevent you slicing all the way through. Repeat with the remaining potatoes.

Sprinkle a little salt over each potato.

Place the potatoes in the prepared tin and roast them for about 45 minutes, turning them every 10 minutes, so they get nice and buttery.

Ten minutes before the end of cooking time, sprinkle the chopped garlic and rosemary into the slits in the potatoes and pop the tin back in the oven.

If you want the potatoes to be extra crispy, cook them for a bit longer.

DAIRY-FREE

Use dairy-free spread or more olive oil instead of the butter.

NASI GORENG

An Indonesian all-in-one rice dish, which introduces your child to amazing Asian flavours. Prawns are a fantastic source of protein, zinc and omega 3. Choose frozen prawns from the North Atlantic – these are the best and cheapest.

SERVES A FAMILY OF 4–5

185g brown basmati rice
1 tbsp sesame oil
4–6 chicken thighs, boneless and skinless, diced
2 tbsp tamari soy sauce
2 heaped tsp coconut sugar or light muscovado sugar
6 spring onions, sliced
1 garlic clove, crushed
½ red chilli, finely sliced, to taste
Small knob of fresh root ginger, peeled and diced
1 tsp Thai fish sauce
100–120g fine green beans, trimmed and cut into 3
1 red pepper, deseeded and finely chopped
Juice of 1 lime
180g frozen prawns, defrosted

To serve:
1 free-range egg omelette, finely sliced
1 tbsp salted peanuts, crushed
1 tbsp fresh coriander leaves, torn
Handful of shop-bought prawn crackers (optional)

Cook the rice according to the packet instructions.

Place a large frying pan over a medium heat, add half the sesame oil and fry the diced chicken with the tamari and coconut sugar until it is cooked through. Remove the chicken from the pan and set aside.

Pour the rest of the sesame oil into the pan and add the spring onions, followed by the garlic, chilli, ginger and fish sauce. Cook for 3–4 minutes then return the chicken to the pan along with the green beans, red pepper, the cooked and drained rice and the lime juice.

Simmer for 2–3 minutes to soften the veg, before stirring in the prawns. These should only take a couple of minutes to heat if they are already cooked.

Serve with sliced omelette, crushed peanuts, coriander leaves and some prawn crackers, as a treat.

ITALIAN FISH & FENNEL STEW

A lovely tomato-based soupy stew with just a hint of fennel to aid digestion. Easy on the tummy, this is a quick lunch or simple supper that you can rustle up from freezer and larder ingredients. Cooked in one saucepan, it's easy on the washing up, too.

SERVES A FAMILY OF 4–5

- 1 tbsp olive oil
- 5 garlic cloves, crushed
- 1 small fennel bulb, trimmed and diced
- 1 carrot, peeled and diced
- 1 celery stick, trimmed and diced
- 1 x 400g tin chopped tomatoes
- 8–10 small waxy potatoes, peeled and halved horizontally
- 500ml fish stock
- 280g cod loin, cubed
- 180g North Atlantic prawns, frozen and defrosted, or fresh
- 50g spinach, finely chopped
- 1 large sprig of parsley, leaves roughly chopped
- ¼ fresh chilli, deseeded and finely chopped (optional)

Place a large saucepan over a medium heat, add the oil and fry the garlic, fennel, carrot and celery for 3–4 minutes.

Add the tomatoes and potatoes with the stock and cook uncovered for 10–15 minutes, or until the potatoes are soft.

Blend the mixture at this point, if you want to disguise the veg for a younger child.

Add the cod and continue to cook for a couple of minutes. Then stir in the prawns and spinach and cook for a further couple of minutes.

Just before serving, sprinkle over the parsley and chilli.

STICKY MISO VENISON
WITH BROWN RICE NOODLES

This is a speedy supper that delivers a whole range of health-promoting nutrients. Iron-rich venison goes beautifully with brightly coloured veg. Miso, made from fermented soybeans, is a gut-friendly food packed with protein and B vitamins.

SERVES A FAMILY OF 4–5

- 250g venison or beef steak, thinly sliced
- 1 tbsp sesame oil, plus extra for frying
- 1 tbsp dark miso paste
- 1 tbsp runny honey
- 1 tbsp rice vinegar
- 5cm knob of fresh root ginger, peeled and finely chopped
- 3–4 spring onions, trimmed and chopped
- ¼ fresh chilli, deseeded and finely chopped (optional)
- 1 red pepper, deseeded and finely sliced
- 120g sugar snap peas, halved
- 120g baby sweetcorn, quartered
- 225g (1 packet) brown rice noodles
- 1½ tbsp Furikake sesame and seaweed sprinkles
- Juice of 1 lime

Marinate the venison in the sesame oil, miso, honey and rice vinegar for a minimum of 20 minutes but preferably for a few hours.

Place a large heavy-based frying pan over a low heat, add a little sesame oil and fry the ginger, spring onions and chilli, if using, gently for a couple of minutes.

Add the meat and its marinade and cook on a high heat for a few more minutes until soft.

Add the red pepper, sugar snap peas and baby sweetcorn and stir-fry until they are tender but still have plenty of crunch.

Meanwhile cook the noodles according to the packet instructions.

Serve the venison with a sprinkling of Furikake seasoning, a big squeeze of lime juice and the brown rice noodles.

CHAPTER SIX

LUNCHBOXES, PICNICS AND SNACKS

SAVOURY SAVIOURS

COURGETTE & PEA FRITTATA

Speedy frittatas are made for Sunday evenings, when you have a house to tidy and school uniform to get ready.

SERVES 4 CHILDREN

4 free-range eggs, beaten
90g Cheddar, grated
Handful of peas (fresh or frozen)
⅓ courgette, finely grated
1 tsp mixed Mediterranean herbs
1 tbsp olive oil, for frying

Mix all the ingredients, except for the oil, together in a bowl and season.

Preheat the oven grill to its highest setting.

Place a small frying pan over a medium heat, add the olive oil and pour in the frittata mixture.

Cook for a couple of minutes on the hob, then pop the pan under the grill to brown the top. This makes the frittata puff up so it is lovely and light.

HERBY LEMON BASHED CHICKEN STRIPS

These zesty goujons are handy for pick-and-mix lunches and buffet suppers.

SERVES 2–4 CHILDREN

2 chicken breasts, skinless
Zest of 1 lemon
2 tbsp mixed Mediterranean herbs
1 tbsp olive oil

Cut the length of one chicken breast, from the side, to create two flat strips. Repeat with the second breast.

Place the slices on some parchment paper and scatter over half the lemon zest and herbs. Season, then turn them over and do the same on the other side.

Cover them with another piece of parchment paper and bash them with a rolling pin to tenderise them.

Place a large frying pan over a medium heat, add the oil and fry the chicken for a few minutes on each side, or until cooked through.

SALMON & POLENTA MUFFINS

If you are struggling to get your kids to eat fish, this might be the recipe for you. A tasty muffin that is super-filling and freezes well, so you can always have some ready to pop in a lunchbox. To boost the nutritional value, add some finely chopped spinach and/or red pepper.

MAKES 12 MUFFINS

Olive oil, for greasing
210g polenta
90g spelt, wholemeal flour
1 tsp baking powder
180g Cheddar, grated
1 salmon steak, steamed and flaked, or 75g smoked salmon pieces
1 tbsp fresh dill, chopped
1 free-range egg
235ml buttermilk or crème fraîche

Preheat the oven to 200°C/180°C fan/gas mark 5/6 and grease a 12-hole muffin tin with oil.

Mix all the ingredients together in a large bowl.

Use an ice cream scoop to dollop the mixture evenly into the muffin tin holes. They do not rise much so fill them up to the top.

Bake them for 25 minutes, or until golden brown and springy to the touch.

EGG-FREE

Replace the egg with a mix of 1 tbsp ground flaxseeds and 2½ tbsp water.

DAIRY-FREE

Use a vegan melting cheese, such as Violife, instead of Cheddar and replace the buttermilk with oat crème fraîche such as Oatly.

GLUTEN-FREE

Use chickpea flour (also known as besan or gram flour).

MACKEREL & SPRING ONION MUFFINS

These nutritious muffins are a brilliant lunchbox filler and a great way to top up your kids' omega 3. They can easily be made a day or two in advance – store them in an airtight container and they will keep for up to two days.

MAKES 8 MUFFINS

- 4 free-range eggs
- 1 spring onion, trimmed and chopped
- 1 tbsp chopped fresh dill
- 1 tbsp chopped fresh parsley
- 1 fillet smoked mackerel, cut into small pieces
- Black pepper

Preheat the oven to 180°C/160°C fan/gas mark 4 and line a muffin tin with 8 paper cases. You could also use an 8-hole silicone muffin tin.

Beat the eggs in a bowl until light and frothy.

Add the spring onion, dill and parsley.

Pour the mixture into the muffin cases and place 2 small pieces of mackerel on top.

Bake the muffins for around 12 minutes, or until they are slightly brown on top and springy to touch. Season with black pepper to taste.

CHICKPEA, BACON & SPRING ONION PANCAKES

Try these gorgeous savoury pancakes made from chickpea flour for a lower-carbohydrate breakfast or lunchbox filler. Swap the bacon for smoked mackerel or smoked salmon to give an omega 3 boost. Or add other vegetables to the mix, such as peas, grated courgette or grated carrot.

MAKES 12–16 PANCAKES

Splash of olive oil for frying each pancake
4 rashers of bacon, finely chopped
180g chickpea (also known as gram or besan) flour or wholemeal flour
470ml water
4 spring onions, trimmed and finely chopped
4 tsp finely chopped fresh parsley

Place a frying pan over a medium heat, add the olive oil and fry the bacon until it is nice and crispy.

Mix the chickpea flour with the water in a large bowl and stir well to remove any lumps.

Add the spring onions and parsley to the bowl, season with salt and black pepper, then let the batter stand for 10 minutes.

Place a large frying pan over a medium heat and coat it lightly with olive oil.

Spoon tablespoonfuls of the pancake mixture into the pan – you can usually fit 3 in at once. Once the surface starts to bubble, flip them over carefully and cook the other side. Serve immediately.

CHINESE FIVE SPICE CHICKEN DRUMSTICKS

Kids love to chomp on chicken drumsticks – pander to their inner caveman!

MAKES 8 DRUMSTICKS
2 tbsp tamari soy sauce
1 tbsp grainy mustard
1 tbsp runny honey
1 tsp Chinese five spice
8 chicken drumsticks

Mix the tamari, mustard, honey and Chinese five spice together in a bowl.

Add the chicken drumsticks to the sticky mixture and mix well, ensuring they get an even coating.

Leave them to marinate for at least 20 minutes (a few hours would be even better).

Preheat the oven to 200°C/180°C fan/gas mark 5/6.

Place the drumsticks on a baking tray and roast them for 35 minutes, or until they are cooked through.

SOYA-FREE
Use coconut aminos or coconut teriyaki sauce instead of tamari soy sauce.

PEAR & SAGE CHICKEN MINI BURGERS

A sage is a wise person, and the herb sage is known to help memory, attention and learning. So use it more in the kitchen to cultivate your own little sages!

MAKES 8 MINI BURGERS

- 2 tbsp olive oil
- 1 small onion, finely chopped
- 6 sage leaves, finely chopped
- 2 chicken breasts, skinless, diced
- 1 firm pear, peeled, cored and grated

Place a small frying pan over a medium heat, add 1 tbsp of the olive oil and fry the onion and sage for a couple of minutes.

Tip the cooked onion mixture into a food processor with the chicken and pear. Season with salt and black pepper and pulse for about a minute, or until the chicken looks like mince.

Shape the chicken mixture into small balls, then flatten them slightly to make them into mini patties.

Place a large frying pan over a medium heat and add the remaining olive oil. Fry the patties gently in the pan for a few minutes on each side, turning them carefully to ensure they are brown all over and cooked through.

Serve them with *My Super-Healthy Ketchup* (see page 135).

GREEN CHICKEN ORBS

These flavoursome little chicken bites are packed with goodness. A quick and mess-free way to boost a lunchbox with protein, iron and folate.

SERVES 2–3 CHILDREN

- 4 tsp olive oil
- 1 small red onion, finely chopped
- ½ courgette, finely grated
- 1 garlic clove, finely chopped
- 1 tsp mixed Mediterranean herbs
- 2 chicken breasts, skinless, diced
- Handful of baby spinach leaves

Place a small frying pan over a medium heat, add 2 tsp of the olive oil and fry the onion and grated courgette for a couple of minutes until soft.

Add the garlic and the herbs and cook for another minute.

Put the chicken in a food processor with the cooked onion mixture and the spinach. Pulse for about a minute, or until the chicken and spinach are finely chopped.

Shape the chicken mixture into small balls, then flatten them slightly to make them into mini patties.

Place a large frying pan over a medium heat and add the rest of the olive oil. Fry the patties gently in the pan for a few minutes on each side, turning them carefully to ensure they are brown all over and cooked through.

Serve them with *My Super-Healthy Ketchup* (see page 135).

CHEESY QUINOA BALLS

A great vegetarian lunchbox option, with protein-packed quinoa.

MAKES 20 BALLS

- 370g cooked and drained quinoa
- 2 tsp mixed Mediterranean herbs
- 1 free-range egg, beaten
- 2 tbsp tomato concentrate
- 115g Cheddar, grated
- ½ medium carrot, peeled and finely grated
- 1 garlic clove, diced

Preheat the oven to 180°C/160°C fan/gas mark 4.

Combine all the ingredients together in a bowl, then shape the mixture into small balls the size of a walnut.

Place the balls on a baking tray and bake them for 25 minutes.

They are delicious hot or cold.

CREAM CHEESE STUFFED VEG
WITH SEEDED SPRINKLES

Turn crunchy vegetable sticks into a more substantial snack.

SERVES 2–3 CHILDREN

- 1–2 celery sticks
- 1–2 thick slices of red pepper
- 1–2 cucumber sticks
- 1–2 thick carrot sticks
- 3 tbsp cream cheese
- 2 tsp flaxseeds or chia seeds

Fill or spread the vegetable sticks with cream cheese and sprinkle the seeds on top.

DAIRY-FREE
Swap the cream cheese for nut or seed butter.

RAINBOW DIPS WITH CRUDITÉS

Kids are more likely to eat veg if they have something delicious to dunk them into. All three of these dips make great sandwich and jacket potato fillings, too. As they are free from dairy, nuts and sesame, they make a great staple for kids with allergies. If you are able to, add a couple of teaspoonfuls of tahini to boost the calcium and iron content.

EACH DIP SERVES 6–8

MINTY PEA DIP

75g cooked petit pois
½ x 400g tin cannellini beans, drained and rinsed
1 large sprig of parsley leaves, chopped
1 large sprig of mint leaves, chopped
1 tbsp olive oil
Juice of ½ lemon
½ garlic clove, finely chopped
Small pinch of fine sea salt

ooooooo

Blend all the ingredients together in a food processor.

PINK BEETROOT DIP

1 x 400g tin butter beans, drained and rinsed
1 small ready-cooked beetroot (vinegar-free)
1 tsp ground cumin
1 tbsp olive oil
Juice of ½ lemon
½ garlic clove, finely chopped
Small pinch of fine sea salt

ooooooo

Blend all the ingredients together in a food processor.

SMOKY SWEET POTATO DIP

1 sweet potato
1 x 400g tin chickpeas, drained and rinsed
1 tsp smoked paprika
1 tbsp olive oil
Juice of ½–1 lemon, to taste
Small pinch of fine sea salt

ooooooo

Preheat the oven to 180°C/160°C fan/ gas mark 4.

Bake the sweet potato for 30–40 minutes, or until it is soft.

Remove the sweet potato from the oven, peel then blend it with all the other ingredients in a food processor.

MINTY PEA DIP
PINK BEETROOT DIP
SMOKY SWEET POTATO DIP

CHEESY SPELT NOUGHTS & CROSSES

A healthier, but no less fun, version of cheese straws with extra fibre. These are great for snacks, picnics and lunchboxes.

MAKES 18 SHAPES

- 150g cold unsalted butter, cut into small cubes
- 250g spelt or wholemeal flour
- 180g Cheddar, grated
- ¼ tsp English mustard powder
- ¼ tsp paprika
- 2 tsp fresh thyme leaves or 1 tsp dried thyme
- 2 tsp ground flaxseeds
- 2 tbsp cold water

Preheat the oven to 190°C/170°C fan/gas mark 5 and line 2 baking trays with parchment paper.

Rub the butter and flour together in a bowl with your finger tips until the mixture resembles breadcrumbs. Add half the cheese, along with the mustard powder, paprika, thyme and flaxseeds.

Stir in 1–2 tablespoonfuls of cold water until the mixture comes together in a ball.

Roll the dough out on a floured surface to about 1cm thick. Slice it into long 1cm-wide strips (try using a pizza slice) that you can shape into noughts and crosses, or use a pastry cutter to make other shapes.

Sprinkle the rest of the cheese over the shapes and transfer them to the prepared baking trays.

Bake them in the oven for 20 minutes, or until they are golden but not brown – otherwise they get a slightly burnt taste.

DAIRY-FREE

Swap the butter for dairy-free spread and the Cheddar for a vegan cheese, such as Violife Prosociano. Reduce the cooking time to 12–15 minutes.

GLUTEN-FREE

Use plain, gluten-free flour.

ZESTY SALMON BALLS

An easy finger food for lunchboxes and picnics that is brimming with omega 3 and vitamin C. These go beautifully with *Omega Mayo* (see page 131) or *My Super-Healthy Ketchup* (see page 135).

MAKES 9–10 BALLS

- 2 salmon steaks, skin removed
- 2 spring onions, trimmed and finely chopped
- 1 free-range egg, beaten
- 1 tbsp spelt, wholemeal or chickpea flour
- Zest of 1 lemon
- 1 sprig of parsley, leaves finely chopped
- 1 tbsp olive oil

Steam or poach the salmon in a covered pan with 100ml water for 10 minutes, then remove the skin.

Flake the salmon flesh into a large bowl and combine it with the other ingredients. Season with salt and black pepper.

Divide the mixture into 9 or 10 balls.

Place a large frying pan over a medium heat, add the oil and fry the salmon balls for about 10 minutes, turning them frequently to ensure they brown all over.

EGG-FREE

Use 1 tbsp ground flaxseeds mixed with 2½ tbsp water.

MACKEREL PÂTÉ

This omega 3-rich pâté can be stuffed into wholemeal pitta breads or eaten as a dip with crudités, oatcakes or rye bread.

SERVES 6–8 CHILDREN

- 200g smoked mackerel
- 100g cream cheese
- Juice of 1 lemon
- 1 tbsp fresh parsley, finely chopped
- 1 tbsp fresh dill, finely chopped
- Black pepper

Strip the skin off the mackerel.

For a smooth pâté, blitz it with the other ingredients in a food processor. Or for a chunkier texture, simply mix it all together with a fork in a bowl.

DAIRY-FREE

Use oat crème fraîche, such as Oatly, instead of cream cheese.

SWEET TREATS

MINI RASPBERRY CHOCOLATE CUPCAKES

Kids just love the chocolate topping and the crunchy oat base of these no-cook cupcakes. Top them with your favourite berries. They make a great speedy snack.

MAKES 16 CUPCAKES

- 100g oats
- 150g pitted dates
- 50g ground almonds
- 120g organic cooking chocolate (dark, milk or white)
- 16 raspberries, to decorate

You will need a 16-hole silicone mini muffin tin, or 16 mini cupcake paper cases.

Blitz the oats, dates and almonds in a food processor for a minute or so until you have a slightly sticky powder.

At the same time, gently melt the chocolate in a bain-marie – a bowl set over a small saucepan of simmering water.

Place a teaspoonful of the oat mixture in each hole of the silicone mini muffin tin.

Drizzle a teaspoonful of the chocolate mixture on top then stick a raspberry in the middle.

Place the muffin tin in the freezer for 20 minutes or in the fridge for 40 minutes to set.

These are best stored in the fridge and eaten within a couple of days.

DAIRY-FREE
Use dairy-free chocolate.

GLUTEN-FREE
Use gluten-free oats.

NUT-FREE
Replace the almonds with 25g extra oats and 25g sunflower seeds.

GINGERBREAD BISCUITS

Making gingerbread biscuits is a great activity to entertain bored children. This recipe uses blackstrap molasses, which is similar to black treacle, and has the lowest sugar content of any sugar product on the market. Molasses is full of iron, calcium and magnesium – all important for growing kids. Cinnamon helps to balance blood sugars and maintain a healthy metabolism.

MAKES 14–16 BISCUITS

- 80g butter, melted
- 1 free-range egg
- 40g blackstrap molasses or treacle
- 40g coconut sugar or light muscovado sugar
- ½ tsp vanilla essence
- 200g spelt or wholemeal flour
- ½ tsp baking powder
- 1 tsp ground cinnamon
- ½ tsp ground ginger
- ¼ tsp mixed spice

Mix the melted butter with the egg, molasses, sugar and vanilla essence in a large bowl.

Combine all the remaining ingredients in a separate bowl, then stir them into the sugar mixture to form a sticky dark dough.

Cover the bowl and chill it in the fridge for about 30 minutes.

Preheat the oven to 180°C/160°C fan/gas mark 4 and line a baking tray with parchment paper.

On a lightly floured surface, roll the dough out to a couple of millimetres thick.

Cut it into shapes and use a spatula to lift them carefully on to the prepared baking tray.

Chill them again in the fridge for about 15 minutes then pop them into the oven for 10–12 minutes.

Leave them to firm up on the tray for a few minutes then transfer them to a wire rack to cool.

DAIRY-FREE

Use dairy-free spread or coconut oil (with a neutral flavour) instead of butter.

GLUTEN-FREE

Use gluten-free flour instead of spelt flour.

EGG-FREE

Mix 1 tbsp ground flaxseeds with 2½ tbsp water to replace the egg.

TAHINI BREAD

This is a totally AMAZING fluffy bread that is suitable for people on a number of 'free-from' diets. Rich in calcium and iron, it goes well with *Raspberry Chia Jam* (see page 191) or *Hazelnut Choc Spread* (see page 190) and is lovely toasted. The bitterness sometimes associated with tahini is not an issue with this bread, so it will appeal to even the fussiest eaters.

MAKES 10–12 SMALL SLICES

- 1 x 300g jar light tahini sesame paste
- 4 free-range eggs
- ½ tsp bicarbonate of soda
- 30ml apple cider vinegar
- 1 tsp fine sea salt
- 1–2 tbsp runny honey
- 1 tbsp pumpkin seeds (optional)

Preheat the oven to 180°C/160°C fan/gas mark 4 and line a 250g loaf tin with parchment paper.

Combine all the ingredients, except for the pumpkin seeds, in a food processor or mix with a spoon in a large bowl.

Pour the mixture into the prepared tin then sprinkle the pumpkin seeds on top for some added crunch.

Bake it for 35–40 minutes, or until it is cooked through and golden.

Leave it to cool in the tin for a few minutes then turn out on to a wire rack to finish cooling before slicing it.

EGG-FREE

Either use egg replacer powder, or combine 4 tbsp ground flaxseeds with 10 tbsp water.

DOUBLE CHOC COOKIE SANDWICHES

A batch of these usually lasts less than half an hour in our household. As well as being crazily delicious, they contain lots of brain-nourishing goodies such as oats, sunflower seeds and coconut oil. A real hit when you have other kids over to play and an easy way to avoid junk-filled shop-bought cookies.

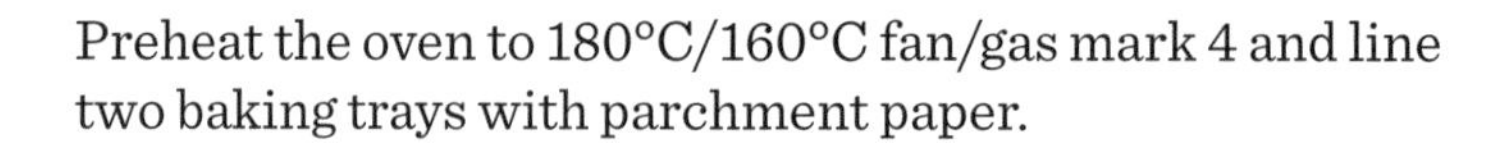

MAKES 20 COOKIES

- 175g oats
- 60g sunflower seeds
- 20g raw cacao powder or cocoa powder
- 40g coconut sugar or light muscovado sugar
- 100ml maple syrup
- 65ml (about 4 tbsp) coconut oil (with a neutral flavour) or 65g butter, melted

Preheat the oven to 180°C/160°C fan/gas mark 4 and line two baking trays with parchment paper.

Blitz the oats and sunflower seeds together in a food processor until you have a flour-like consistency. Use a grinder blade if your processor has one.

Tip this mixture into a large bowl and stir in the cacao powder and sugar, followed by the maple syrup and melted coconut oil.

Combine the ingredients to form a ball. If the coconut oil was still warm, place the dough in the fridge for 10–15 minutes to cool down.

Place the dough ball between two pieces of parchment paper and roll it out to the thickness of a pound coin. Use a round cookie cutter (approx. 5cm in diameter) to cut out 20 circles.

Transfer them to the baking trays and bake the cookies in the oven for 11–12 minutes, removing them before they begin to brown.

Leave them to firm up on the trays for a few minutes, then transfer to a wire rack to cool completely.

Once cool, sandwich two cookies together with *Hazelnut Choc Spread* (see page 190). They also taste amazing with *Raspberry Nana Nice-Cream* in the middle (see page 192).

HAZELNUT CHOC SPREAD

This is hazelnut spread without the rubbish. Guilt-free bliss that you can slap between biscuits, stir into porridge or spread on toast. This is an absolute must for your fridge at all times!

oooooooo

MAKES 10–15 SERVINGS

200g hazelnuts
4 tbsp maple syrup
4 tsp coconut oil (with a neutral flavour)
4 tbsp raw cacao powder or cocoa powder
½ tsp vanilla essence
Pinch of fine sea salt
100ml hazelnut milk

Preheat the oven to 170°C/150°C fan/gas mark 3.

Tip the hazelnuts onto a baking tray and roast them in the oven for 10 minutes.

Remove them from the oven and wrap them in a tea towel. Rub them roughly to remove some of their skins.

Blitz them in a food processer for 8–10 minutes, or until you have a smooth hazelnut butter.

With the processor still on, slowly add all the other ingredients.

Store in a sealed jar – the spread will keep refrigerated for up to 2 weeks.

NUT-FREE

Use toasted sunflower seeds instead of hazelnuts, and coconut milk or rice milk instead of hazelnut milk.

RASPBERRY CHIA JAM

Free from refined and fake sugars, this jam is a doddle to make and tastes fabulous. Try making it with blackcurrants or blackberries to ring the changes.

MAKES 10–12 SERVINGS
300g frozen raspberries
2 tbsp runny honey
2 tbsp chia seeds

Place a saucepan over a low heat, add all the ingredients and cook gently for 5 minutes, or until the berries have broken down into a pulp.

Pour the jam into a warm glass jar and leave it to thicken up for 10 minutes.

It can be stored in the fridge for up to 10 days.

RASPBERRY NANA NICE-CREAM

This is a perfect way to use up overripe bananas that have become soft and speckled. Bananas can be stored in the freezer for several months so never throw overripe ones away. Every child and grown-up who has tasted this has absolutely loved it and asked for more. Spread some between two *Double Choc Cookies* (see page 188) for a heavenly treat.

SERVES 4–5 CHILDREN

- 3 overripe bananas, peeled and chopped into 3 or 4 pieces
- 200g raspberries (fresh or frozen)

Put the bananas in a sealed plastic bag in the freezer for at least 2 hours.

Ten minutes before you are ready to eat, take them out of the freezer so they defrost slightly.

Blitz them with the raspberries in a food processor for 2–3 minutes, or until they have blended together into a thick, dark pink paste. You may need to scrape down the sides of the processor a couple of times to get the fruit to blend, if the bananas are still quite frozen.

Eat it immediately or refreeze it for another time.

COURGETTE BROWNIES

Everyone loves a brownie and these can be eaten with zero guilt as they contain courgette and pecans and are free from refined sugar. They freeze beautifully and defrost very quickly so you can grab a couple out of the freezer as you are leaving for the afternoon school run and they will be ready to eat by pick-up.

MAKES 16 BROWNIES

- 150g unsalted butter
- 150g dark cooking chocolate
- 3 free-range eggs
- 125g coconut sugar or light muscovado sugar
- ½ courgette, finely grated
- 125g spelt or brown rice flour
- 1 tsp vanilla essence
- ¼ tsp fine sea salt
- 100g pecans, crushed (optional)

Preheat the oven to 180°C/160°C fan/gas mark 4 and line a 22cm square baking tin with parchment paper.

Place a saucepan over a low heat, add the butter and chocolate and melt gently, stirring occasionally.

Meanwhile, beat the eggs and coconut sugar together in a bowl with an electric whisk, then add the courgette.

Stir in the chocolate mixture, before folding in the flour, vanilla essence, salt and pecans, if using.

Pour the brownie mixture into the prepared tin and bake it in the oven for 25 minutes – it should be springy on top and slightly squidgy in the middle.

Remove it from the oven and put the tin on a wire rack and leave to cool, before cutting the brownie into 16 pieces.

DAIRY-FREE
Use 150g coconut oil (with a neutral flavour) or dairy-free spread instead of butter.

EGG-FREE
Use 3 tbsp ground flaxseeds mixed with 7½ tbsp water.

NUT-FREE
Use mixed seeds instead of pecans.

GOOEY SEEDED FLAPJACKS

With no refined sugar, these are still gorgeously soft and sweet. You can cut back on the honey and dates each time you make them as your kids become accustomed to less sweetness.

MAKES 16 FLAPJACKS

- 100g set honey
- 100g butter
- 100g pitted dates, chopped
- 50ml water
- 200g rolled oats
- 30g sunflower seeds
- 30g pumpkin seeds

Preheat the oven to 180°C/160°C fan/gas mark 4 and line a 22cm square baking tin with parchment paper.

Place a saucepan over a medium heat, add the honey, butter, pitted dates and water and stir until the butter has melted and the dates are soft.

Remove from the heat and purée the mixture in a blender.

Tip the purée into a large bowl, then stir in the oats and seeds.

Spread the mixture evenly in the prepared tin and bake it for 20–25 minutes, or until it is golden brown.

Leave it to cool before cutting it into squares.

DAIRY-FREE

Use a dairy-free spread, such as Biona, or coconut oil (with a neutral flavour).

GLUTEN-FREE

Use gluten-free oats or buckwheat flakes.

BLONDIE CRISPIES

My daughter's favourite sweet treat, these delicious caramel crispies only take a couple of minutes to make.

MAKES 24 CRISPIES

4 tbsp coconut oil (with a neutral flavour)
4 tbsp cashew nut butter
4 tbsp set honey
125g wholegrain brown rice crispies*
24 blueberries or raspberries, to decorate

* You can use popped quinoa or a 50:50 mix of popped quinoa and brown rice crispies, if you prefer.

Arrange 24 mini cupcake cases on a baking tray.

Place a saucepan over a low heat, add the coconut oil, cashew nut butter and honey and melt gently. Set aside a small amount of this mixture, which you will use to stick the blueberries to the crispies (about 1 heaped tbsp).

Stir in the brown rice crispies, ensuring they get an even coating. Spoon the mixture into the mini cupcake paper cases.

Dip the berries in the remaining sauce and stick one on top of each crispie.

Put the tray in the fridge for 30–40 minutes to set.

These can be stored in the fridge – eat them within a couple of days.

NUT-FREE

Use sunflower seed butter or tahini paste instead of cashew nut butter.

SPELT LEMON POPPY SEED COOKIES

These contain much less sugar than shop-bought biscuits but are just as sweet tasting. The poppy seeds add an extra crunch as well as a mineral boost. These cookies freeze really well so you could make double the quantity and keep half for another day.

MAKES 18–20 COOKIES

- 350g spelt or wholemeal flour
- 60g coconut sugar or light muscovado sugar
- ½ tsp bicarbonate of soda
- 10g poppy seeds
- Pinch of fine sea salt
- Zest of 2 lemons
- 125g unsalted butter
- 60g set honey
- 1 free-range egg, lightly beaten

Preheat the oven to 170°C/150°C fan/gas mark 3 and line 2–3 baking trays with parchment paper.

Mix all the dry ingredients and lemon zest together in a large bowl.

Melt the butter and honey slowly in a saucepan over a low heat.

Stir the butter mixture into the dry ingredients, add the beaten egg and combine everything well.

Use your hands to roll the cookie mixture into a large ball.

Roll 18–20 walnut-sized balls of the mixture and place them on the prepared baking trays about 1½–2cm apart. Press each ball down lightly with a fork, so they are flat and about ½ cm thick. Bake them for 13–15 minutes, or until they are golden.

Remove them from the oven and leave them to firm up on the baking trays for a few minutes, then use a spatula to transfer them carefully on to a wire rack to cool and harden.

GLUTEN-FREE

Use 350g plain gluten-free flour or 300g gluten-free flour plus 50g ground almonds.

DAIRY-FREE

Use a dairy-free spread, such as Biona, or coconut oil (with a neutral flavour).

EGG-FREE

Use 1 tbsp ground flaxseeds mixed with 2½ tbsp water.

STRAWBERRY POPCORN

A movie night isn't the same without popcorn. This is quick to make and much cheaper and healthier than the ready-made stuff.

SERVES 3–4 CHILDREN

75g popping maize/ corn kernels
2 tbsp butter, ghee or coconut oil (with a neutral flavour)
1 tbsp coconut sugar or light muscovado sugar
5g freeze-dried strawberry pieces*

* You will find freeze-dried strawberry and raspberry pieces in the baking section of large supermarkets.

Place a saucepan over a medium heat, add the corn kernels and cover with a lid. Leave the kernels to pop, giving the pan a shake occasionally.

Meanwhile, place a separate large saucepan over a low heat and melt the butter.

Toss the popcorn and sugar into the butter, cover with a lid and give it a good shake.

Remove from the heat and leave it to cool for about 5 minutes.

Tip into a serving bowl, scatter with the strawberry pieces and tuck in!

MANGO CASHEW CREAMS

Only two simple ingredients: cashews and mango. You can't get easier than that. These little puddings are creamy, sweet and filling. They are also incredibly nourishing and combine healthy protein, fats, fibre and natural fruit sugar. No gluten, dairy, eggs or soya in sight.

MAKES 4 PUDDINGS

- 125g cashews
- Pinch of fine sea salt
- 2 large mangoes, peeled and stoned
- 1 tsp flaxseeds, to sprinkle (optional)

Soak the cashews in water for 2 hours with the salt.

Blitz 1 of the mangoes in a blender for 45 seconds. Pour the purée into a small jug.

Drain the cashews and put them in the blender with the other mango. Blitz them together for 45 seconds or so until you have a smooth mixture.

Spoon the cashew mango mixture into 4 ramekins and then pour some of the plain mango purée on top.

Sprinkle some flaxseeds on top and serve. These can be stored in the fridge for 3–4 days.

NUT-FREE

Mix the mango with plain Greek yoghurt or coconut yoghurt.

RASPBERRY & PEAR CRUMBLE

A warm, nourishing pudding that we often have for Sunday lunch in early autumn, when raspberries and pears are at their best.

SERVES 4–5 CHILDREN

Crumble topping:
75g spelt or wholemeal flour
75g oats
75g butter, at room temperature
50g coconut sugar or light muscovado sugar
10g pumpkin seeds
10g sunflower seeds

Fruit filling:
4 pears, peeled, cored and cut into small chunks
150–200g raspberries (fresh or frozen)

Preheat the oven to 180°C/160°C fan/gas mark 4.

Combine all the topping ingredients by rubbing them together to form a chunky crumble mixture. You can also use a food processor to do the work for you.

If the pears are a bit hard, place a small saucepan over a medium heat and cook them for 10 minutes, or until soft. Otherwise, mix them with the raspberries straight away in the bottom of a pie dish.

Sprinkle the crumble topping evenly over the fruit.

Bake the crumble for 25–30 minutes, or until the topping is nice and brown.

DAIRY-FREE
Replace the butter with coconut oil (with a neutral flavour) or dairy-free spread.

GLUTEN-FREE
Use gluten-free plain flour and oats.

ELDERFLOWER & BERRY ICE LOLLIES

On a hot day there is nothing better than a refreshing ice lolly to help you cool down.

MAKES 6–8 LOLLIES

200ml apple and elderflower juice (or 190ml cloudy apple juice and 10ml elderflower cordial, mixed)
Handful of mixed berries

Put 3–4 berries in each hole of an ice lolly mould. Fill the hole with juice and pop the ice lolly sticks in.

Freeze for 3–4 hours.

WATERMELON PIZZA

Your kids will love making these themselves. Get them to decorate their watermelon pizzas with their favourite fruit, nuts and seeds.

MAKES 6–8 PIZZAS

- 1–2 slices of watermelon, about 2cm thick and deseeded
- 200g mixed berries or other fruit
- Squeezy chocolate sauce, such as Sweet Freedom Choc Shot
- 1 tsp seeds of your choice (optional)

Cut each watermelon slice into wedge-shaped pieces.

Top with berries or other fruit and seeds of your choice and squirt on the chocolate sauce.

BANANA BOATS

A snack that can be whipped up in an instant for hungry tummies.

SERVES 3 CHILDREN

- 3 bananas, peeled and halved lengthways
- 3 tbsp crunchy peanut butter, almond butter or cashew nut butter
- 12–15 mixed berries, apple or orange slices

Spread peanut butter on the flat side of the banana halves and then pop some berries or fruit slices on top.

NUT-FREE

Use cream cheese or tahini instead.

WEEKLY MENU PLANNER – WEEK 1

	MONDAY	TUESDAY	WEDNESDAY
Breakfast	Blueberry & Banana Muffin (p.77) *with* Strawberry & Honey Kefir (p.96)	Hazelnut Choc Porridge (p.72–4)	Peanut Butter & Sliced Strawberries on Sourdough Toast (p.90)
Mid-morning Snack	Olives & Cherry Tomatoes	Carrot Sticks *with* Pink Beetroot Dip (p.174)	Seeded Oatcakes *with* Cream Cheese
Lunch	Chinese Five Spice Chicken Drumsticks (p.169) Cucumber & Cheese Wholemeal Pitta Grapes	Herby Lemon Bashed Chicken Strips (p.163) Rice Salad Hardboiled Egg Cherry Tomatoes Pineapple Slices	Chickpea, Bacon & Spring Onion Pancakes (p.168) Seeded Oatcakes Minty Pea Dip (p.174) *with* Celery & Cucumber Sticks Blueberries & Sunflower Seeds
After-school	Gooey Seeded Flapjacks (p.196)	Gingerbread Biscuits (p.184)	Banana Boats (p.206)
Snack/Tea Supper	Black Bean Chilli *with* Mango & Strawberry Salsa (p.152)	Haddock & Salmon Fish Pie (p.139) *with* Peas	Chicken Noodle Miso Soup (p.113)

THURSDAY	FRIDAY	SATURDAY	SUNDAY
Overnight Berry Bircher Oats (p.80)	Granola (p.66) *with* Greek Yoghurt *plus* Apple, Cinnamon & Flax Compote (p.68)	Carrot & Poppy Seed Waffles (p.78)	Smoky Sausage, Egg & Beans (p.87)
Grapes with Cheddar Cubes Mackerel & Spring Onion Muffins (p.167)	Pumpkin Seeds & Raspberries Pear and Sage Chicken Mini Burgers (p.170)	Banana Peanut Butter Sandwich *with* Proper Hot Chocolate (p.104)	Watermelon & Mint Slushy (p.100)
Red Lentil, Pepper & Tomato Soup (p.110) Seeded Oatcakes Mango Slices	Egg and Cress Mayo Wrap Olives, Halloumi Strips & Watermelon Chunks	Chinese Ginger Chicken with Brown Rice Noodles (p.136)	Five Veg Shepherd's Pie (p.120) Courgette Brownies (p.194)
Raspberry Chia Smoothie (p.95)	Blondie Crispies (p.197)	Double Choc Cookie Sandwiches (p.188) *with* Hazelnut Choc Spread *or* Raspberry Nana Ice-Cream	Tahini Bread (p.186) *with* Raspberry Chia Jam (p.191)
Crunchy Lemon Chicken Goujons *with* Omega Mayo Smart Sweet Potato Chips (p.128–131) Sugar Snap Peas	Turmeric Kedgeree (p.123)	Nasi Goreng (p.156)	Chicken, Chorizo & Flageolet Stew (p.154) *with* Hasselback Potatoes (p.155) Broccoli

WEEKLY MENU PLANNER – WEEK 2

	MONDAY	TUESDAY	WEDNESDAY
Breakfast	Green Egg & Ham Muffin (p.84)	Granola (p.66) *with* Greek Yoghurt & Mixed Berry Compote (p.68)	Crunchy Breakfast Pebbles (p.82) *with* Milk & Blueberries
Mid-morning Snack	Blueberries & Toasted Seeds	Smoky Sweet Potato Dip & Cucumber (p.174)	Cream Cheese Stuffed Veg (p.173)
Lunch	Cheesy Quinoa Balls (p.173) Pearled Farro Comfort Soup (p.109) Kiwi Fruit	Salmon & Polenta Muffins (p.164) Cream Cheese, Banana, Cinnamon & Honey Toast (p.90) Red Pepper Slices Apple	Courgette & Pea Frittata (p.163) Chicken Pasta Pesto with Fresh Tomatoes (p.126) Strawberries
After-school	Mini Raspberry Chocolate Cupcakes (p.183)	Spelt Lemon Poppy Seed Cookies (p.198)	Mango Cashew Creams (p.202)
Snack/Tea Supper	Falafel Three Ways (p.148) *with* Tzatziki, Fruity Feta Salad (p.147) Wholemeal Pitta Breads	Chicken & Thyme Meatballs with a Red Pepper Sauce & Spaghetti (p.150) *with* Mixed Salad	Creamy Haddock & Sweetcorn Chowder (p.108)

THURSDAY	FRIDAY	SATURDAY	SUNDAY
Cinnamon Toast (p.81) *with* Mango & Passionfruit Kefir (p.96)	Berry Nice Porridge (p.72–4)	Egg & Salmon Mini Roll-ups (p.88)	Brain-Boost Pancakes (p.71) *with* Sliced Banana & Maple Syrup
Pear & Cheddar Cubes	Cream Cheese Stuffed Dates	Elderflower & Berry Ice Lolly (p.205)	Zingy Carrot Juice (p.102)
Zesty Salmon Balls (p.178) *with* Omega Mayo (p.131) Cheesy Spelt Noughts & Crosses (p.177) Carrot Sticks Watermelon Gazpacho (p.114)	Green Chicken Orbs (p.172) Mackerel Pâté (p.180) *with* Pittas Cucumber & Olives Banana	Veg-loaded Beef Bolognaise (p.121) *with* Mixed Salad	Sticky Miso Venison with Brown Rice Noodles (p.159) Raspberry & Pear Crumble (p.203)
Green Monster Smoothie (p.95)	Watermelon Pizza (p.206)	Strawberry Popcorn (p.200)	Sourdough Toast *with* Hazelnut Choc Spread (p.190)
Chicken & Spinach Curry *with* Brown Rice & Mini Poppadums (p.142)	Fishy Fridays (p.132) *with* Cheesy Courgette Chips (p.134) & My Super-healthy Ketchup (p.135)	Pulled Duck (p.145) *with* Persian Coleslaw & Pomegranate Cauliflower Couscous (p.146)	Mini Toad in the Hole (p.118) *with* Broccoli

SHOPPING LIST

Some people like to buy just what they need for specific recipes, while others prefer to stock up on basic ingredients. Here is a list of goodies we often have in our fridge, freezer or store cupboard:

Fresh and frozen vegetables: broccoli, cabbage (red, white and spring), cauliflower, courgettes (zucchini), green beans, kale (and kalettes), mange tout, mushrooms, pak choi, peas, runner beans, sugar snap peas, spinach.

Root vegetables: carrots, celeriac, garlic, leeks, onions (white, red and spring), parsnips, potatoes (white, sweet and new), pumpkin, shallots, squash, swedes, turnips.

Salad: avocado, celery, cress, cucumber, fennel, lettuce (lamb's, Romaine, Little Gem), pea shoots, peppers (bell), radishes, rocket, spinach (baby leaf), tomato, watercress.

Fresh and frozen fruit: apples, apricots, bananas, blueberries, currants (red, black), cherries, grapes, kiwis, lemons, limes, mandarins, mangoes, melons (honeydew, cantaloupe, galia), nectarines, papayas, passionfruits, peaches, pears, pineapples, plums, pomegranates, oranges, raspberries, satsumas, strawberries, watermelons.

Dried fruit: apple rings, apricots (unsulphured), banana chips, cranberries (unsweetened), dates, figs, goji berries, mulberries, mangoes, prunes.

Healthy grains: barley, corn, maize, polenta (choose organic), couscous (wholegrain), farro, kamut, millet, oats, wheat (bulgur, freekah or wholemeal), rice (wholegrain brown, black, red or wild), spelt.

Noodles: pasta (wholemeal, spelt, buckwheat, chickpea, lentil, quinoa), noodles (brown rice, soba buckwheat).

Flours: spelt, buckwheat, chickpea (also known as besan/gram), Dove's Farm gluten-free, rye, ground almonds, coconut, quinoa, brown rice, wholemeal.

Baking ingredients: baking powder, bicarbonate of soda, xanthum gum, arrowroot.

Cereals: porridge oats, puffed brown rice, puffed quinoa, buckwheat flakes, millet flakes, brown rice flakes, coconut flakes.

Pseudo-grains: buckwheat, quinoa.

Beans and pulses: lentils (red, green, puy), beans (butter, flageolet, edamame, cannellini, black, mung, adzuki, kidney), chickpeas, yellow split peas.

Fish: line-caught mackerel, anchovies, sardines, wild or organic salmon, trout, cod, halibut.

Poultry and meat: organic/free-range poultry (chicken, turkey, duck, pheasant, partridge, guinea fowl), organic/free-range/grass-fed lamb, beef, pork, venison.

Broths and stocks: fresh meat/poultry/fish/vegetable stock; Marigold Yeast Free or Steenbergs Vegetable Bouillon.

Milk: organic full-fat cow's, goat's, oat milk, nut milks (coconut, almond, hazelnut, cashew), hemp milk.

Cheese: organic cow's, goat's, sheep's; buffalo mozzarella.

Yoghurt: Greek, full-fat organic; nut alternatives (coconut, almond, cashew).

Cream: organic crème fraîche, organic cream, oat crème fraîche, such as Oatly.

Eggs: organic free-range chicken's; quail, duck or goose.

Seeds: pumpkin, sunflower, hemp, chia, sesame, flax (linseed), poppy.

Nuts: almonds, pecans, brazils, hazelnuts, walnuts, pistachios, macademias, cashews, pine kernels, peanuts.

Nut butters: peanut, hazelnut, cashew, almond.

Healthy fats: coconut oil (kids prefer cooking coconut oils with a neutral flavour such as Tiana or Biona), olive oil (light and extra virgin), cold-pressed rapeseed oil, organic butter, avocado oil, goose fat, duck fat.

Natural sweeteners: honey (organic, Jarrh, Manuka, local or raw), maple syrup, coconut sugar, black strap molasses, date syrup, dates, vanilla essence, cinnamon, apple, pear or mango purée, mashed banana, stevia (Truvia), xylitol (Perfect Sweet/Xylitol).

Chocolate: dark 70% chocolate, raw cacao powder and nibs, carob, dairy-free brands such as Moo Free or Om.

Fresh and dried herbs: mint, parsley, coriander, rosemary, thyme, sage, oregano, basil, mixed Mediterranean herbs, Herbes de Provence.

Ground and whole spices: turmeric, black pepper, cumin, coriander, ginger, fenugreek, cardamom, cloves, sumac, paprika.

Seaweeds: nori, kombu, dulse, seaweed salad.

Salt: Himalayan pink, sea and celery.

Preserved foods: olives in olive oil or brine, capers, sun-dried tomatoes.

Condiments: miso, tahini, tamari soy sauce, organic tomato concentrate, mustard, Biona Worcester sauce, organic mayonnaise, Biona egg-free mayonnaise, coconut aminos.

Vinegars: apple cider, balsamic, apple balsamic, red and white wine.

Superfood powders: acai, baobab, fruits (strawberry, raspberry, banana).

Hot drinks: herbal teas including chamomile, fresh mint, peppermint, ginger, liquorice and rooibos.

You should be able to source most of these foods in your local supermarket. However, some of the allergen-friendly and specialist foods may be a bit trickier to find. We have therefore compiled a list of suppliers on www.naturedoc.clinic/thegoodstuff, where you will also find an up-to-date list of kitchen equipment and resources that we find helpful.

1. Monteiro, C., Moubarac, J., Levy, R., Canella, D., Louzada, M. & Cannon, G. (2018). Household availability of ultra-processed foods and obesity in nineteen European countries. *Public Health Nutrition*, 21(1), 18-26. DOI: 10.1017/S1368980017001379
2. Soliman, A., De Sanctis, V. & Elalaily, R. (2014). Nutrition and pubertal development. *Indian Journal of Endocrinology and Metabolism*, 18(Suppl 1), S39–S47. doi.org/10.4103/2230-8210.145073
3. Obesity Statistics. *House of Commons Briefing Paper*, 20th March 2018. researchbriefings.parliament.uk/ResearchBriefing/Summary/SN03336
4. How sugar affects our kids. www.nhs.uk/change4life/food-facts/sugar#vkrDZFrY1ZThvs7K.97
5. Results of the UK National Diet and Nutrition Survey (NDNS) 2018. assets.publishing.service.gov.uk/government/uploads/system/uploads/attachment_data/file/699241/NDNS_results_years_7_and_8.pdf
6. British parents giving up on convincing kids to eat fruit and vegetables, survey finds. www.independent.co.uk/life-style/food-and-drink/news/healthy-eating-children-fruit-vegetables-five-a-day-families-nutrition-diet-a8344601.html
7. Steck, S., Shivappa, N., Tabung, F., Harmon, E., Brook & Wirth, Michael & Hurley, Thomas & Hebert, James & Sc.D. (2014). The dietary inflammatory index: a new tool for assessing diet quality based on inflammatory potential. *The Digest*. 49. 1-9.
8. Rauber, F. et al. Consumption of ultra-processed food products and its effects on children's lipid profiles: A longitudinal study. *Nutrition, Metabolism and Cardiovascular Diseases* , Volume 25, Issue 1 , 116 – 122
9. Aguayo-Patrón, S. V. & Calderón de la Barca, A. M. (2017). Old fashioned vs. ultra-processed-based current diets: possible implication in the increased susceptibility to type 1 diabetes and celiac disease in childhood. *Foods*, 6(11), 100. doi.org/10.3390/foods6110100
10. Diabetes UK comments on rise in type 2 diabetes in children. www.diabetes.org.uk/about_us/news/type-2-diabetes-in-children
11. Fiolet, T., Srour, B., Sellem, L., Kesse-Guyot, E., Allès, B., Méjean, C., ... Touvier, M. (2018). Consumption of ultra-processed foods and cancer risk: results from NutriNet-Santé prospective cohort. *The BMJ*, 360, k322. doi.org/10.1136/bmj.k322
12. Subramaniapillai, M., Carmona, N. E., Rong, C., & McIntyre, R. S. (2017). Inflammation: opportunities for treatment stratification among individuals diagnosed with mood disorders. *Dialogues in Clinical Neuroscience*, 19(1), 27–36.
13. Miller, A. H., & Raison, C. L. (2016). The role of inflammation in depression: from evolutionary imperative to modern treatment target. *Nature Reviews*. Immunology, 16(1), 22–34. doi.org/10.1038/nri.2015.5
14. Khandaker, G. M., Pearson, R. M., Zammit, S., Lewis, G., & Jones, P. B. (2014). Association of serum interleukin 6 and c-reactive protein in childhood with depression and psychosis in young adult life: a population-based longitudinal study. *JAMA Psychiatry*, 71(10), 1121–1128. doi.org/10.1001/jamapsychiatry.2014.1332
15. Patalay, P. & Fitzsimons, E. (2017). Mental ill-health among children of the new century: trends across childhood with a focus on age. *Centre for Longitudinal Studies*. www.cls.ioe.ac.uk/shared/get-file.ashx?itemtype=document&id=3338
16. Arvidsson, L., Eiben, G., Hunsberger, G., De Bourdeaudhuij, I., Molnar, D., Jilani, H., Thumann, B., Veidebaum, T., Russo, P., Tornatitis, M., Santaliestra-Pasías, A. M., Pala, V. & Lissner, L. (2017). Bidirectional associations between psychosocial well-being and adherence to healthy dietary guidelines in European children: prospective findings from the IDEFICS study. *BMC Public Health*, 17 (1) doi.org/10.1186/s12889-017-4920-5
17. Conner, T. S., Brookie, K. L., Richardson, A. C. & Polak, M. A. (2015). On carrots and curiosity: Eating fruit and vegetables is associated with greater flourishing in daily life. Br J Health Psychol, 20: 413-427. DOI: 10.1111/bjhp.12113
18. White, B. A., Horwath, C. C. & Conner, T. S. (2013). Many apples a day keep the blues away – Daily experiences of negative and positive affect and food consumption in young adults. *Br J Health Psychol*, 18: 782-798. DOI: 10.1111/bjhp.12021
19. Conner, T. S., Brookie, K. L., Carr, A. C., Mainvil, L. A. & Vissers, M. C. M. (2017). Let them eat fruit! The effect of fruit and vegetable consumption on psychological well-being in young adults: A randomized controlled trial. *PLoS ONE*, 12(2), e0171206. doi.org/10.1371/journal.pone.0171206
20. Johnson, S. B., Blum, R. W. & Giedd, J. N. (2009). Adolescent maturity and the brain: The promise and pitfalls of neuroscience research in adolescent health policy. *The Journal of Adolescent Health*, 45(3), 216–221. doi.org/10.1016/j.jadohealth.2009.05.016
21. Veg Facts: A briefing by the Food Foundation. (2016). foodfoundation.org.uk/wp-content/uploads/2016/11/FF-Veg-Doc-V5.pdf
22. Holley, C. E., Farrow, C. & Haycraft, E. (2017). A systematic review of methods for increasing vegetable consumption in early childhood. *Current Nutrition Reports*, 6(2), 157–170. doi.org/10.1007/s13668-017-0202-1
23. De Filippis, F., Pellegrini, N., Vannini, L. et al. High-level adherence to a Mediterranean diet beneficially impacts the gut microbiota and associated metabolome. *Gut*, 2016;65:1812-1821.
24. Ramsay, S. A., Shriver, L. H. & Taylor, C. A. Variety of fruit and vegetables is related to preschoolers' overall diet quality. *Preventive Medicine Reports,* Volume 5, 2017, Pages 112-117, ISSN 2211-3355, doi.org/10.1016/j.pmedr.2016.12.003
25. Myles, I. A. (2014). Fast food fever: reviewing the impacts of the Western diet on immunity. *Nutrition Journal*, 13, 61. doi.org/10.1186/1475-2891-13-61
26. Sanchez, A., Reeser, L., Lau, J. & S., Yahiku, H. & Y., Willard, P. & E., McMillan, R. & J., Cho, P. & Y., Magie, S. & R., Register, A. & D., U. (1973). Role of sugars in human

neutrophilic phagocytosis. *The American Journal of Clinical Nutrition*. 26. 1180-4. 10.1093/ajcn/26.11.1180

27. Khan, T. A. & Sievenpiper, J. L. (2016). Controversies about sugars: results from systematic reviews and meta-analyses on obesity, cardiometabolic disease and diabetes. *European Journal of Nutrition*, 55(Suppl 2), 25–43. doi.org/10.1007/s00394-016-1345-3
28. Foster-Powell, K., Holt S. H. A. & Brand-Miller, J. C. (2002). International table of glycemic index and glycemic load values. *The American Journal of Clinical Nutrition*, Volume 76, Issue 1, 1 July 2002, Pages 5–56, doi.org/10.1093/ajcn/76.1.5
29. Di Nicolantonio, J. J., Berger, A. (2016). Added sugars drive nutrient and energy deficit in obesity: a new paradigm. *Open Heart*, 2016;3:e000469. DOI: 10.1136/openhrt-2016-000469
30. Yu, C.-J., Du, J.-C., Chiou, H.-C., Feng, C.-C., Chung, M.-Y., Yang, W., ... Chen, M.-L. (2016). Sugar-sweetened beverage consumption is adversely associated with childhood attention deficit/hyperactivity disorder. *International Journal of Environmental Research and Public Health*, 13(7), 678. doi.org/10.3390/ijerph13070678
31. Knüppel, A., Shipley, M. J., Llewellyn, C. H. & Brunner, E. J. (2017). Sugar intake from sweet food and beverages, common mental disorder and depression: prospective findings from the Whitehall II study. *Scientific Reports*, 7, 6287. doi.org/10.1038/s41598-017-05649-7
32. Diabetes: the basics. www.diabetes.org.uk/diabetes-the-basics
33. Bjerregaard, L., Jensen, B. W., Ängquist, L., Osler, M., Sørensen, T. I. A., Baker, J. L. (2018). Change in overweight from childhood to early adulthood and risk of type 2 diabetes. *N Engl J Med*, 378:1302-1312 DOI: 10.1056/NEJMoa1713231
34. Aller, E. E. J. G., Abete, I., Astrup, A., Martinez, J. A. & van Baak, M. A. (2011). Starches, sugars and obesity. *Nutrients*, 3(3), 341–369. doi.org/10.3390/nu3030341
35. Glycemic Index for sweeteners. www.sugar-and-sweetener-guide.com/glycemic-index-for-sweeteners.html
36. University of Rhode Island. (2010, March 25). Pure maple syrup contains medicinally beneficial compounds, pharmacy researcher finds. *ScienceDaily*. Retrieved July 19, 2018 from www.sciencedaily.com/releases/2010/03/100321182924.htm
37. Dearlove, R. P., Greenspan, P., Hartle, D. K., Swanson, R.B. & Hargrove, J. L. (2008). Inhibition of protein glycation by extracts of culinary herbs and spices. *J Med Food*,11(2):275-81. DOI: 10.1089/jmf.2007.536
38. Bernardo, M. A., Silva, M. L., Santos, E., Moncada, M. M., Brito, J., Proença, L., ... de Mesquita, M. F. (2015). Effect of cinnamon tea on postprandial glucose concentration. *Journal of Diabetes Research*, 2015, 913651. doi.org/10.1155/2015/913651
39. Baum, J. I., Gray, M. & Binns, A. (2015). Breakfasts higher in protein increase postprandial energy expenditure, increase fat oxidation, and reduce hunger in overweight children from 8 to 12 years of age. *The Journal of Nutrition*, Volume 145, Issue 10, 1 October 2015, Pages 2229–2235, doi.org/10.3945/jn.115.214551
40. Edefonti, V., Rosato, V., Parpinel, M., Nebbia, G., Fiorica, L., Fossali, E., Ferraroni, M., Decarli, A., Agostoni, C.(2014). The effect of breakfast composition and energy contribution on cognitive and academic performance: a systematic review. *The American Journal of Clinical Nutrition*, Volume 100, Issue 2, 1 August 2014, Pages 626–656, doi.org/10.3945/ajcn.114.083683
41. Swanson, D., Block, R. & Mousa, S. A. (2012). Omega-3 fatty acids EPA and DHA: Health benefits throughout life. *Advances in Nutrition*, 3(1), 1–7. doi.org/10.3945/an.111.000893
42. Kuratko, C. N., Barrett, E. C., Nelson, E. B. & Norman, S. (2013). The relationship of docosahexaenoic acid (DHA) with learning and behavior in healthy children: A review. *Nutrients*, 5(7), 2777–2810. doi.org/10.3390/nu5072777
43. Montgomery, P., Burton, J. R., Sewell, R. P., Spreckelsen, T. F. & Richardson, A. J. (2013). Low blood long chain omega-3 fatty acids in UK children are associated with poor cognitive performance and behavior: A cross-sectional analysis from the DOLAB study. *PLoS ONE*, 8(6), e66697. doi.org/10.1371/journal.pone.0066697
44. Stonehouse, W. (2014). Does consumption of LC omega-3 PUFA enhance cognitive performance in healthy school-aged children and throughout adulthood? Evidence from clinical trials. *Nutrients*, 6(7), 2730–2758. doi.org/10.3390/nu6072730
45. Richardson, A. J., Burton, J. R., Sewell, R. P., Spreckelsen, T. F. & Montgomery, P. (2012). Docosahexaenoic acid for reading, cognition and behavior in children aged 7–9 years: A randomized, controlled trial (The DOLAB Study). *PLoS ONE*, 7(9), e43909. doi.org/10.1371/journal.pone.0043909
46. Königs, A. & Kiliaan, A. J. (2016). Critical appraisal of omega-3 fatty acids in attention-deficit/hyperactivity disorder treatment. *Neuropsychiatric Disease and Treatment*, 12, 1869–1882. doi.org/10.2147/NDT.S68652
47. Hibbeln, J. R. & Gow, R. V. (2014). Omega-3 fatty acid and nutrient deficits in adverse neurodevelopment and childhood behaviors. *Child and Adolescent Psychiatric Clinics of North America*, 23(3), 555–590. doi.org/10.1016/j.chc.2014.02.002
48. Montgomery, P., Burton, J. R., Sewell, R. P., Spreckelsen, T. F. & Richardson, A. J. (2014). Fatty acids and sleep in UK children: subjective and pilot objective sleep results from the DOLAB study – a randomized controlled trial. *Journal of Sleep Research*, 23(4), 364–388. doi.org/10.1111/jsr.12135
49. Benbrook, C. M., Butler, G., Latif, M. A., Leifert, C. & Davis, D. R. (2013). Organic production enhances milk nutritional quality by shifting fatty acid composition: A United States-wide, 18-month study. *PLoS ONE*, 8(12), e82429. doi.org/10.1371/journal.pone.0082429
50. Driscoll, C. T., Mason, R. P., Chan, H. M., Jacob, D. J., & Pirrone, N. (2013). Mercury as a global pollutant: Sources, pathways, and effects. *Environmental Science & Technology*, 47(10), 4967–4983. doi.org/10.1021/es305071v
51. Eckel, R. H.. (2015). Eggs and beyond: is dietary cholesterol no longer important? *The American Journal of Clinical Nutrition*, Volume 102, Issue 2, 1 August 2015, Pages 235–236, doi.org/10.3945/ajcn.115.116905
52. Oyi, A.R. & Onaolapo, Josiah & Obi, R.C. (2010). Formulation and antimicrobial studies of coconut (cocos nucifera linne) oil. *Research Journal of Applied Sciences, Engineering and Technology*, 2. 133-137.

53. *Healthline*: 12 Proven benefits of avocado. https://www.healthline.com/nutrition/12-proven-benefits-of-avocado
54. Koletzko, B., Human milk lipids. *Ann Nutr Metab*, 2016;69(suppl 2):27-40 doi.org/10.1159/000452819
55. Ratnayake, W.M., L'Abbe, M.R., Farnworth, S., Dumais, L., Gagnon, C., Lampi, B., Casey, V., Mohottalage, D., Rondeau, I., Underhill, L., Vigneault, M., Lillycrop, W., Meleta, M., Wong, L. Y., Ng, T., Gao, Y., Kwong, K., Chalouh, S., Pantazopoulos, P., Gunaratna, H., Rahardja, A., Blagden, R., Roscoe, V., Krakalovich, T., Neumann, G., Lombaert, G. A. Trans fatty acids: current contents in Canadian foods and estimated intake levels for the Canadian population. *J AOAC Int.* 2009 Sep-Oct;92(5):1258-76. PubMed PMID: 19916364.
56. Ginter, E., Simko, V. New data on harmful effects of trans-fatty acids. DOI: 10.4149/BLL_2016_048
57. Mazidi, M., Gao, H. & Kengne, A. P. (2017). Inflammatory markers are positively associated with serum trans-fatty acids in an adult American population. *Journal of Nutrition and Metabolism*, 2017, 3848201. doi.org/10.1155/2017/3848201
58. Valdes, A. M., Walter, J., Segal, E. & Spector, T. D. (2018). Role of the gut microbiota in nutrition and health. *The BMJ*, 361, k2179. doi.org/10.1136/bmj.k2179
59. Johnston, C. S. & Gaas, C. A. (2006). Vinegar: medicinal uses and antiglycemic effect. *Medscape General Medicine*, 8(2), 61.
60. Ezz El-Arab, A. M., Girgis, S. M., Hegazy, E. M. & Abd El-Khalek, A. B. (2006). Effect of dietary honey on intestinal microflora and toxicity of mycotoxins in mice. *BMC Complementary and Alternative Medicine*, 6, 6. doi.org/10.1186/1472-6882-6-6
61. Suez, J., Korem, T., Zilberman-Schapira, G., Segal, E. & Elinav, E. (2015). Non-caloric artificial sweeteners and the microbiome: findings and challenges. *Gut Microbes*, 6(2), 149–155. doi.org/10.1080/19490976.2015.1017700
62. Swithers, S. E.. (2015). Artificial sweeteners are not the answer to childhood obesity. *Appetite*, Volume 93, 2015, Pages 85-90, ISSN 0195-6663, doi.org/10.1016/j.appet.2015.03.027
63. Irwin, S. V., Fisher, P., Graham, E., Malek, A., Robidoux, A. (2017) Sulfites inhibit the growth of four species of beneficial gut bacteria at concentrations regarded as safe for food. P*LOS ONE*, 12(10): e0186629. doi.org/10.1371/journal.pone.0186629
64. Chassaing, B., Koren, O., Goodrich, J., Poole, A., Srinivasan, S., Ley, R. E. & Gewirtz, A. T. (2015). Dietary emulsifiers impact the mouse gut microbiota promoting colitis and metabolic syndrome. *Nature*, 519(7541), 92–96. doi.org/10.1038/nature14232
65. Holder, M. K., Chassaing, B. (2018). Impact of food additives on the gut-brain axis. *Physiology & Behavior*, Volume 192, 2018, Pages 173-176, ISSN 0031-9384, doi.org/10.1016/j.physbeh.2018.02.025
66. Zhang, N., Ju, Z. & Zuo, T. (2018). Time for food: The impact of diet on gut microbiota and human health. *Nutrition*, Volumes 51–52, 2018, Pages 80-85, ISSN 0899-9007, doi.org/10.1016/j.nut.2017.12.005
67. Steck, S., Shivappa, N., Tabung, F., Harmon, E., Brook & Wirth, Michael & Hurley, Thomas & Hebert, James & Sc.D. (2014). The dietary inflammatory index: A new tool for assessing diet quality based on inflammatory potential. *The Digest*. 49. 1-9.
68. Sand, J. (2005). A short history of MSG. *Gastronomica*, Vol. 5 No. 4, Fall 2005; (pp. 38-49) DOI: 10.1525/gfc.2005.5.4.38
69. Zhou, Y. & Danbolt, N. C. (2014). Glutamate as a neurotransmitter in the healthy brain. *Journal of Neural Transmission*, 121(8), 799–817. doi.org/10.1007/s00702-014-1180-8
70. Haroon, E., Miller, A. H. (2017). Inflammation effects on brain glutamate in depression: Mechanistic considerations and treatment implications. *Curr Top Behav Neurosci*, 2017;31:173-198. DOI: 10.1007/7854_2016_40
71. Bermudo-Soriano, C. R., Perez-Rodriguez, M. M., Vaquero-Lorenzo, C. & Baca-Garcia, E. (2012). New perspectives in glutamate and anxiety. *Pharmacology Biochemistry and Behavior*, Volume 100, Issue 4, 2012, Pages 752-774, ISSN 0091-3057, doi.org/10.1016/j.pbb.2011.04.010
72. Naaijen, J. et al. Striatal structure and its association with N-Acetylaspartate and glutamate in autism spectrum disorder and obsessive compulsive disorder. *European Neuropsychopharmacology*, Volume 28 , Issue 1 , 118 – 129
73. Pittenger, C., Bloch, M. H. & Williams, K. (2011). Glutamate abnormalities in obsessive compulsive disorder: Neurobiology, pathophysiology, and treatment. *Pharmacology & Therapeutics*, 132(3), 314–332. doi.org/10.1016/j.pharmthera.2011.09.006
74. Holton, K. F. & Cotter, E. W. (2018). Could dietary glutamate be contributing to the symptoms of obsessive-compulsive disorder? *Future Science OA*, 4(3), FSO277. doi.org/10.4155/fsoa-2017-0105
75. Arain, M., Haque, M., Johal, L., Mathur, P., Nel, W., Rais, A., ... Sharma, S. (2013). Maturation of the adolescent brain. *Neuropsychiatric Disease and Treatment*, 9, 449–461. doi.org/10.2147/NDT.S39776
76. Teng, J., Zhou, W., Zeng, Z., Zhao, W., Huang, Y., Zhang, X. Quality components and antidepressant-like effects of GABA green tea. doi.org/10.1039/c7fo01045a
77. Amsterdam, J. D., Li, Y., Soeller, I., Rockwell, K., Mao, J. J. & Shults, J. (2009). A randomized, double-blind, placebo-controlled trial of oral *matricaria recutita* (chamomile) extract therapy of generalized anxiety disorder. *Journal of Clinical Psychopharmacology*, 29(4), 378–382. doi.org/10.1097/JCP.0b013e3181ac935c
78. Oh, S.-H., Moon, Y.-J. & Oh, C.-H. (2003). γ-aminobutyric acid (GABA) content of selected uncooked foods. *Preventive Nutrition and Food Science*. 8. 10.3746/jfn.2003.8.1.075
79. Selhub, E. M., Logan, A. C. & Bested, A. C. (2014). Fermented foods, microbiota, and mental health: ancient practice meets nutritional psychiatry. *Journal of Physiological Anthropology*, 33(1), 2. doi.org/10.1186/1880-6805-33-2
80. *Scientific American*: What is the difference between artificial and natural flavors? www.scientificamerican.com/article/what-is-the-difference-be-2002-07-29/
81. Cantwell, M. & Elliott, C. (2017). Nitrates, nitrites and nitrosamines from processed meat intake and colorectal cancer risk. *J Clin Nutr Diet*, 3:27. DOI: 10.4172/2472-1921.100062

82. Hord, N. G., Tang, Y., Bryan, N. S.. (2008). Food sources of nitrates and nitrites: the physiologic context for potential health benefits. *The American Journal of Clinical Nutrition*, Volume 90, Issue 1, 1 July 2009, Pages 1–10, doi.org/10.3945/ajcn.2008.27131
83. Food for thought. *The Pesticide Action Network*. http://www.pan-uk.org/food-for-thought/
84. Ozen, S., Goksen, D. & Darcan, S. Chapter Two – Agricultural pesticides and precocious puberty. Editor(s): Litwack, G., *Vitamins & Hormones*, Academic Press, Volume 94, 2014, Pages 27-40, ISSN 0083-6729, ISBN 9780128000953, doi.org/10.1016/B978-0-12-800095-3.00002-X
85. Liu, J. & Schelar, E. (2012). Pesticide exposure and child neurodevelopment: summary and implications. *Workplace Health & Safety*, 60(5), 235–243. DOI: 10.3928/21650799-20120426-73
86. Rauh, V. A., Perera, F. P., Horton, M. K., Whyatt, R. M., Bansal, R., Hao, X., ... Peterson, B. S. (2012). Brain anomalies in children exposed prenatally to a common organophosphate pesticide. *Proceedings of the National Academy of Sciences of the United States of America*, 109(20), 7871–7876. doi.org/10.1073/pnas.1203396109
87. Velmurugan, G., Ramprasath, T., Swaminathan, K., Mithieux, G., Rajendhran, J., Dhivakar, M., ... Ramasamy, S. (2017). Gut microbial degradation of organophosphate insecticides-induces glucose intolerance via gluconeogenesis. *Genome Biology*, 18, 8. doi.org/10.1186/s13059-016-1134-6
88. *Diabetologia*: Small study suggests consuming large amounts of artificial sweeteners may increase risk of developing type 2 diabetes. www.sciencedaily.com/releases/2017/09/170913193141.htm
89. Hill, S. E., Prokosch, M.L., Morin, A. & Rodeheffer, C. D. (2014). The effect of non-caloric sweeteners on cognition, choice, and post-consumption satisfaction. *Appetite*, Volume 83, 2014, Pages 82-88, ISSN 0195-6663, doi.org/10.1016/j.appet.2014.08.003
90. *NHS Choices*: The truth about aspartame www.nhs.uk/live-well/eat-well/aspartame-facts/
91. Yılmaz, S. & Uçar, A. (2014). A review of the genotoxic and carcinogenic effects of aspartame: does it safe or not? *Cytotechnology*, 66(6), 875–881. doi.org/10.1007/s10616-013-9681-0
92. Mueller, N. T., Jacobs, D. R., MacLehose, R. F., Demerath, E. W., Kelly, S. P., Dreyfus, J. G. & Pereira, M. A. (2015). Consumption of caffeinated and artificially sweetened soft drinks is associated with risk of early menarche. *The American Journal of Clinical Nutrition*, 102(3), 648–654. doi.org/10.3945/ajcn.114.100958
93. Ashok, I. & Sheeladevi, R. (2014). Biochemical responses and mitochondrial mediated activation of apoptosis on long-term effect of aspartame in rat brain. *Redox Biology*, 2, 820–831. doi.org/10.1016/j.redox.2014.04.011
94. Humphries, P., Pretorius, E. & Naudé, H. (2007). Direct and indirect cellular effects of aspartame on the brain. *European Journal Of Clinical Nutrition*, 2007/08/08/online dx.doi.org/10.1038/sj.ejcn.1602866
95. Bian, X., Chi, L., Gao, B., Tu, P., Ru, H. & Lu, K. (2017). The artificial sweetener acesulfame potassium affects the gut microbiome and body weight gain in CD-1 mice. *PLoS ONE*, 12(6), e0178426. doi.org/10.1371/journal.pone.0178426
96. Cong, W., Wang, R., Cai, H., Daimon, C. M., Scheibye-Knudsen, M., Bohr, V. A., ... Martin, B. (2013). Long-term artificial sweetener acesulfame potassium treatment alters neurometabolic functions in C57BL/6J mice. *PLoS ONE*, 8(8), e70257. doi.org/10.1371/journal.pone.0070257
97. Nettleton, J. E., Reimer, R. A., Shearer, J. (2016). Reshaping the gut microbiota: Impact of low calorie sweeteners and the link to insulin resistance? *Physiology & Behavior*, Volume 164, Part B, 2016, Pages 488-493, ISSN 0031-9384, doi.org/10.1016/j.physbeh.2016.04.029
98. Griffiths, C. et al. A five year longitudinal study investigating the prevalence of childhood obesity: comparison of BMI and waist circumference. *Public Health*, Volume 127, Issue 12, 1090 – 1096
99. Lundahl, A., Kidwell, K. M & Nelson, T. D. (2014). Parental underestimates of child weight: A meta-analysis. *Pediatrics*, Feb 2014, peds.2013-2690; DOI: 10.1542/peds.2013-2690
100. Rauber, F., Louzada, M. L. da C., Steele, E. M., Millett, C., Monteiro, C. A. & Levy, R. B. (2018). Ultra-processed food consumption and chronic non-communicable diseases-related dietary nutrient profile in the UK (2008–2014). *Nutrients*, 10(5), 587. doi.org/10.3390/nu10050587
101. Krajmalnik-Brown, R., Ilhan, Z.-E., Kang, D.-W. & DiBaise, J. K. (2012). Effects of gut microbes on nutrient absorption and energy regulation. nutrition in clinical practice. *Official Publication of the American Society for Parenteral and Enteral Nutrition*, 27(2), 201–214. doi.org/10.1177/0884533611436116
102. Schwartz, B. S., Pollak, J., Bailey-Davis, L., Hirsch, A. G., Cosgrove, S. E., Nau, C., ... Bandeen-Roche, K. (2016). Antibiotic use and childhood body mass index trajectory. *International Journal of Obesity*, 40(4), 615–621. doi.org/10.1038/ijo.2015.218
103. Kalliomäki, M., Collado, M. C., Salminen, S. & Isolauri, E. (2008). Early differences in fecal microbiota composition in children may predict overweight. *The American Journal of Clinical Nutrition*, Volume 87, Issue 3, 1 March 2008, Pages 534–538, doi.org/10.1093/ajcn/87.3.534
104. Greer, R. L., Dong, X., Moraes, A. C. F., Zielke, R. A., Fernandes, G. R., Peremyslova, E., ... Shulzhenko, N. (2016). Akkermansia muciniphila mediates negative effects of IFNγ on glucose metabolism. *Nature Communications*, 7, 13329. doi.org/10.1038/ncomms13329
105. *Nature Medicine*: A purified membrane protein from Akkermansia muciniphila or the pasteurized bacterium improves metabolism in obese and diabetic mice. dx.doi.org/10.1038/nm.4236
106. Cani, P. D., Dao, M. C., Everard, A., Aron-Wisnewsky, J. et al. (2016). Akkermansia muciniphila and improved metabolic health during a dietary intervention in obesity: Relationship with gut microbiome richness and ecology. *Gut* 2016;65:426-436.
107. Anhê, F. F., Pilon, G., Roy, D., Desjardins, Y., Levy, E. & Marette, A. (2016). Triggering Akkermansia with dietary polyphenols: A new weapon to combat the metabolic syndrome? *Gut Microbes*, 7(2), 146–153. doi.org/10.1080/19490976.2016.1142036

108. Chodkowski B. A., Cowan, R. L. & Niswender, K. D. (2016). Imbalance in resting state functional connectivity is associated with eating behaviors and adiposity in children. *Heliyon*, 2016; 2 (1): e00058 DOI: 10.1016/j.heliyon.2015.e00058
109. Spiegel, K., Tasali, E., Leproult, R. & Van Cauter, E. (2009). Effects of poor and short sleep on glucose metabolism and obesity risk. *Nature Reviews*. Endocrinology, 5(5), 253–261. doi.org/10.1038/nrendo.2009.23
110. Liu, J., Hanlon, A., Ma, C., Zhao, S. R., Cao, S. & Compher, C. (2014). Low blood zinc, iron, and other sociodemographic factors associated with behavior problems in preschoolers. *Nutrients*, 6(2), 530–545. doi.org/10.3390/nu6020530
111. Black, M. M. (2012). Integrated strategies needed to prevent iron deficiency and to promote early child development. *Journal of Trace Elements in Medicine and Biology*: Organ of the Society for Minerals and Trace Elements (GMS), 26(0), 120–123. doi.org/10.1016/j.jtemb.2012.04.020
112. Tauman, R., Avni, H., Drori-Asayag, A., Nehama, H., Greenfeld, M. & Leitner, Y. (2017). Sensory profile in infants and toddlers with behavioral insomnia and/or feeding disorders. *Sleep Medicine*, Volume 32, 2017, Pages 83-86, ISSN 1389-9457, doi.org/10.1016/j.sleep.2016.12.009
113. Mura Paroche, M., Caton, S. J., Vereijken, C. M. J. L., Weenen, H. & Houston-Price, C. (2017). How infants and young children learn about food: A systematic review. *Frontiers in Psychology*, 8, 1046. doi.org/10.3389/fpsyg.2017.01046
114. Anagnostou, K., Meyer, R., Fox, A. & Shah, N. (2015). The rapidly changing world of food allergy in children. *F1000Prime Reports*, 7, 35. doi.org/10.12703/P7-35
115. Braun-Fahrländer, C. *Therapeutische Umschau* (2013), 70, pp. 714-719. doi.org/10.1024/0040-5930/a000469
116. Foong, R.-X., Meyer, R., Dziubak, R., Lozinsky, A. C., Godwin, H., Reeve, K., ... Shah, N. (2017). Establishing the prevalence of low vitamin D in non-immunoglobulin-E mediated gastrointestinal food allergic children in a tertiary centre. *The World Allergy Organization Journal*, 10(1), 4. doi.org/10.1186/s40413-016-0135-y
117. Maathuis, A., Havenaar, R., He, T. & Bellmann, S. (2017). Protein digestion and quality of goat and cow milk infant formula and human milk under simulated infant conditions. *Journal of Pediatric Gastroenterology and Nutrition*, 65(6), 661–666. doi.org/10.1097/MPG.0000000000001740
118. Seward, H., Meyer, R. & Shah, N. (2017). Iodine Status and Growth in Cow's Milk Allergy. *Journal of Pediatric Gastroenterology and Nutrition*. 64(5):655–656, MAY 2017 DOI: 10.1097/MPG.0000000000001511
119. Antvorskov, J. C., Josefsen, K., Engkilde, K., Funda, D. P. & Buschard, K. (2014). Dietary gluten and the development of type 1 diabetes. *Diabetologia*, 57(9), 1770–1780. doi.org/10.1007/s00125-014-3265-1
120. Badsha, H. (2018). Role of diet in influencing rheumatoid arthritis disease activity. *The Open Rheumatology Journal*, 12, 19–28. doi.org/10.2174/1874312901812010019
121. Liontiris M.I. & Mazokopakis E.E. (2017). A concise review of Hashimoto thyroiditis (HT) and the importance of iodine, selenium, vitamin D and gluten on the autoimmunity and dietary management of HT patients. Points that need more investigation. *Hell J Nucl Med*. 2017 Jan-Apr;20(1):51-56. DOI: 10.1967/s002449910507
122. Ohry, A. & Tsafrir, J. (1999). Is chicken soup an essential drug? *Canadian Medical Association Journal*, 161(12), 1532–1533.
123. Karuppiah, P. & Rajaram, S. (2012). Antibacterial effect of Allium sativum cloves and Zingiber officinale rhizomes against multiple-drug resistant clinical pathogens. *Asian Pacific Journal of Tropical Biomedicine*, 2(8), 597–601. doi.org/10.1016/S2221-1691(12)60104-X
124. Guo, Y. (2014). Experimental study on the optimization of extraction process of garlic oil and its antibacterial effects. *African Journal of Traditional, Complementary, and Alternative Medicines*, 11(2), 411–414.
125. Mandal, M. D. & Mandal, S. (2011). Honey: its medicinal property and antibacterial activity. *Asian Pacific Journal of Tropical Biomedicine*, 1(2), 154–160. doi.org/10.1016/S2221-1691(11)60016-6
126. Simonyi, A., Chen, Z., Jiang, J., Zong, Y., Chuang, D. Y., Gu, Z., ... Sun, G. Y. (2015). Inhibition of microglial activation by elderberry extracts and its phenolic components. *Life Sciences*, 128, 30–38. doi.org/10.1016/j.lfs.2015.01.037
127. Krawitz, C., Mraheil, M. A., Stein, M., Imirzalioglu, C., Domann, E., Pleschka, S. & Hain, T. (2011). Inhibitory activity of a standardized elderberry liquid extract against clinically-relevant human respiratory bacterial pathogens and influenza A and B viruses. *BMC Complementary and Alternative Medicine*, 11, 16. doi.org/10.1186/1472-6882-11-16
128. Tiralongo, E., Wee, S. S. & Lea, R. A. (2016). Elderberry supplementation reduces cold duration and symptoms in air-travellers: A randomized, double-blind placebo-controlled clinical trial. *Nutrients*, 8(4), 182. doi.org/10.3390/nu8040182
129. Go to my website www.naturedoc.clinic/thegoodstuff for the recipe for Elderberry Syrup.
130. *J Microbiol Biotechnol*. 2018 Jun 28;28(6):893-901. DOI: 10.4014/jmb.1804.04001
131. Wang, Y., Li, X., Ge, T., Xiao, Y., Liao, Y., Cui, Y., ... Zhang, T. (2016). Probiotics for prevention and treatment of respiratory tract infections in children: A systematic review and meta-analysis of randomized controlled trials. *Medicine*, 95(31), e4509. doi.org/10.1097/MD.0000000000004509
132. Wacker, M. & Holick, M. F. (2013). Sunlight and vitamin D: A global perspective for health. *Dermato-Endocrinology*, 5(1), 51–108. doi.org/10.4161/derm.24494
133. Vitamin D. Information for healthcare professionals www.gov.uk/government/news/phe-publishes-new-advice-on-vitamin-d

INDEX

Recipe page references are in **bold.**

ACKNOWLEDGEMENTS

Writing *The Good Stuff* has taught me that it takes a whole village to bring a book to life. Enormous thanks go to Rebecca Nicolson, Aurea Carpenter Evie Dunne and Paul Bougourd at Short Books for encouraging me to write and develop my dream book. I could not have imagined having a more thoughtful and helpful publisher. I am in gratitude to Deborah Gray who loved my blog so much that she nudged Short Books to get this book written – thank you!

Lovely Millie Pilkington, as ever your child photography skills blow me away. How lucky I am to have known you since we were 18. Thank you for your never-ending enthusiasm.

Alex and Emma Smith thank you for the wonderful book design and stunning recipe shots. Your brilliant team: Andrew Burton, Emily Jonzen, Olivia Wardle and Jo Roberts-Miller were invaluable and so inspiring. Thank you for gathering together Lily, Oscar, Israar, Amara, Eden and Finn for such fun photos.

A big shout out also goes to Daniela Exley, Lottie Brook and team Hastings: Ruby-Rose, Floyd, Raven, Amaro, Nancy, Lucy and Rufus.

Barney, Lara and Charlie you three have given me such joy and inspiration. I love being your mummy! Please keep healthy, happy and well forever.

Darling Christopher, thank you for all your reassurance and love and for keeping me on track, we are simply the best team ever.

Tilly, Poppy, Daisy and Rafi, thank you for trying my recipes and being the best nephew and nieces. Love also goes to George and Catriona for all your support. My mum Libbets and Margaret were two very special women in my life, and both shaped my journey into the world of health in their own very special ways. I miss you both every day.

Huge thanks go to my wonderful NatureDoc practitioners: Jo, Susie, Emma, Arabella and Lucy. Without you I would never have had the time to write this book.

Sarah, you are my rock, I could not imagine NatureDoc without you. Nina thanks for being the most amazing support to Sarah and for keeping NatureDoc.shop ship-shape. Eleanor, thanks for keeping me and my team sane and for being the best sister-in-law I could ask for.

Huge thanks also go to Hugh Fearnley-Whittingstall, Amelia Freer and Liz Earle for all your wise words of encouragement.

One of my greatest thank you's is to the parents and families I have supported over the years. I am immensely humbled to have been entrusted in guiding you through your families' health ups and downs. Your children are a tribute to the hard work you put in every day, and I admire you more than you could ever know. Three cheers to you all!

Lucinda Miller is the founder of NatureDoc, and runs busy clinics across the UK specialising in childhood nutrition. She has been practising as a naturopathic iridologist and herbalist for 20 years, and has also qualified in Functional Medicine. She is a mother of three and lives with her family in Wiltshire.